BARBECUE COOKBOOK

CAVENDISH HOUSE

CONTENTS

Edited by Ruth Farnsworth
Designed by Carol Collins

Published by Marshall Cavendish
Books Limited
58 Old Compton Street,
London W1V 5PA

© Marshall Cavendish Limited 1972,
1973, 1975, 1976, 1977, 1982

First printing 1977 (softback)
Revised and updated edition 1982
    (hardback)

Printed in Italy

ISBN 0 85685 901 X

Weights and Measures

Abbreviations

tbs = tablespoon
tsp = teaspoon
ml = millilitre
l = litre
g = gram
oz = ounce
lb = pound

Note: You will find two systems of measurement given in the recipes. The first is metric; the second, British Imperial. Dry ingredients not given in grams refer to those which can be measured in ml spoon sizes, e.g., 1 tbs = 1 x 15 ml spoon. Make sure you only work with one set of figures; never combine different systems.

INTRODUCTION

Barbecues are one of the most popular and entertaining forms of outdoor cookery. The appeal of barbecues arises not just from the superb flavour that they produce but from their flexibility. Assuming it's not blowing a gale or a blizzard, you can have a barbecue virtually any time and any place — for everyday family cooking, for large gatherings of friends, for the unexpected guest, for children's birthday parties, for supper, lunch, even for breakfast; in town or country, garden or patio, at the beach, at a campsite or picnic ground, even on the deck of a boat. The attraction is so strong that cold-climate dwellers are now beginning to have barbecue fire-places installed in the home.

Barbecues provide financial gain, too. More and more increasingly, barbecue food stands are featuring at local fairs and fêtes and the long lines of people who wait for the open-fire delights testify to their success.

Barbecue basics

Meat cooked over an open fire — what could taste more delicious? The word barbecue, from the French *barbe ā queue*, means to spit roast an animal from its head or 'beard' (*barbe*) to its tail (*queue*); in other words, to roast the entire beast. It is said that this method of cooking was introduced by the French bucanneers who explored North America in the seventeenth century. The other theory is that it was a French term for the open-fire cooking of the Indians.

Below: Have a barbecue to entertain friends.

Choosing a barbecue

Barbecues span from the simplest grill placed on bricks to highly sophisticated electric or gas models. With some good advice from a bricklayer or your local do-it-yourself shop you can improvise your own built-in barbecue; otherwise, there is a very wide range to choose from in the shops.

Manufactured barbecues fall into two categories: charcoal-fuelled and gas or electric types.

The barbecue you choose depends upon how often you plan to use it, how much food you are likely to be cooking and the space in your 'barbecue area'.

Charcoal barbecues
Folding grills are lightweight, easy to clean and store. They are ideal for preparing small amounts of food and travel well in the back of a car.

Bucket grills are portable and compact. Occasionally the grill has a skillet on the other side which makes frying possible.

Portable braziers, large and small, have round or square metal bowls set on legs, usually with wheels. The advantage is that they can be moved easily, which is particularly useful in unpredictable weather. The grill can be raised or lowered, and some come equipped with hoods that act as wind shields. Rotisserie attachments are usually available.

Hibachis come in two sizes — table-top and the double-grilled model. Table-top hibachis are small portable cast-iron buckets with grills. They are ideal for snacks and hors d'oeuvres but unsuitable for large cuts of meat. Double-grilled hibachis are also portable and cast-iron. They are equipped with two wooden-handled adjustable grills, and because of their size can be placed in an empty fire-place for indoor barbecues in the cold months.

Gas and electric barbecues
Even though more expensive than the average charcoal models, gas and electric barbecues are an unquestionable boon to the frequent outdoor cook. Their most notable advantage is the speed with which they work — you simply light the burner or pull the switch and within a matter of minutes the cooking can begin. There is none of the waiting, fanning and watching that is all part of getting a charcoal fire going, nor is there the problem of dealing

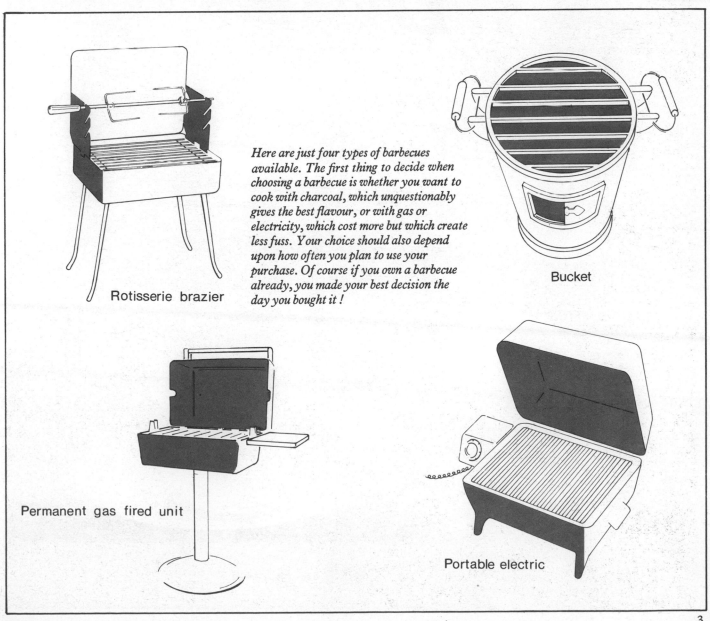

Here are just four types of barbecues available. The first thing to decide when choosing a barbecue is whether you want to cook with charcoal, which unquestionably gives the best flavour, or with gas or electricity, which cost more but which create less fuss. Your choice should also depend upon how often you plan to use your purchase. Of course if you own a barbecue already, you made your best decision the day you bought it!

Rotisserie brazier

Bucket

Permanent gas fired unit

Portable electric

with ashes when 'the party is over'.

Size and shape. Gas and electric barbecues come in roughly the same range as the large portable charcoal braziers. Size, however, can vary tremendously. Some models have as much as .46 square metres / 5 square feet of cooking space.

Fuel supplies. An electric barbecue is simply plugged into a socket but be sure to place it within easy access of an outlet. Gas barbecues run on either bottled propane or butane which lasts for at least ten barbecues or natural gas. The bottled-gas types have fittings built into the barbecue and the containers need replacing when the gas runs out. Barbecues that run on natural gas are either plumbed permanently into the ground to link up with a mains supply or have a hose to connect it to the gas. Your dealer will advise you on these points.

Long-life briquettes. To ensure that the traditional barbecue flavour and quality is imparted to the meat, the manufacturers of gas and electric barbecues supply lava-based briquettes or perforated ceramic tiles. These are called radiants and, when heated through, give the direct heat characteristic of charcoal, with the difference that they last practically forever. To protect them from fat drippings, the manufacturers have devised all sorts of clever systems: chiefly fat-drainage networks and self-cleaning properties. Brochures cover these features in detail.

Other added features. As if the self-cleaning mechanism is not enough, the deluxe gas and electric barbecues have even more attractions, such as adjustable racks (and frequently two or three), storage shelves and double burners, whereby only one needs to be lit when

cooking small amounts. In the United States, where meat used to be hickory smoked, the smoker/meat moisturizer is becoming a very popular device. This is a shallow metal tray with a barrier dividing it in half: water is put in one side and hickory (or other wood) chips in the other. The tray is placed on the radiants and when the water and chips are heated through, a hickory-smelling vapour is produced to impart its fragrance to the meat which sits on a rack above it.

Below: A built-in brick barbecue.

Mastering the coals

Meat and fish are not getting any cheaper and you do not want to throw money down the drain by serving them up as 'burnt offerings'; nor do you want to alienate your friends by doing so. With a little bit of thought and attention, you can be in complete control of a charcoal fire.

Lighting the fire
Starting a fire on an electric or gas barbecue requires no special technique other than pulling a switch or lighting a burner. Not so with a charcoal barbecue; this is not to say that it is difficult, but here are a few basic guidelines:

1. Aim for an even temperature throughout the coals, and this means not just the coals directly beneath the meat, but the coals at least 5 cm / 2 in at either side of it.

2. First lay twisted newspaper or kindling wood, side by side, into the base of the 'bowl'. On top of the kindling place a pyramid-shaped mound of charcoal.

3. Light the kindling, and soon the edges of the charcoal will turn grey. (To encourage a good flame at the start, sprinkle a tiny amount of methylated spirit over the charcoal. Avoid chemical firelighters as these will taint the flavour of the meat being used.

4. After about ten or fifteen minutes, start flattening the mound of charcoal, but make sure that the briquettes stay together so that the fire spreads efficiently from coal to coal.

5. Continue to spread the ashen briquettes so that they will be outside the meat area.

6. Where gaps occur between coals, add more but only in the gaps.

7. The fire is ready, in the daytime, when the coals are grey and, in the evening, when they produce a soft red glow.

Flare-ups
These are the flames that shoot up from the coals when meat fat drips onto them. Uncontrolled, these flames will burn your food to a crisp so try to prevent them from happening. The first precaution is never to put meat on the barbecue when the coals are producing flames.

Another wise move is to trim meat of excess fat before cooking it. If flare-ups still occur, do not despair — just sprinkle the flames with a little water, being careful to confine it to the flame area only. Too much water can drown the coals and put the fire out altogether.

Regulating heat
Again, simple on a gas or electric, as both have heat-regulating knobs, but not quite as easy with charcoal. Here are some tips:
To reduce heat:
1. Move the grill to a higher level.
2. Spread the coals out further.
3. Make a circular well in the coals under the meat to decentralize the heat.

To increase heat:
1. Lower the grill.
2. Open vents to increase draughts.
3. Move the coals closer together.
4. Add more briquettes, being sure to add them to the sides of the burning coals — never on top.

The grill
To get the most out of your barbecue grill, coat it with vegetable oil before cooking, and always wash it immediately after use. If it is really covered with food particles, soak it overnight. Otherwise, just give it a thorough wipe. The most important thing to avoid is leaving it unattended, which only results in food hardening to it and being difficult, if not impossible, to remove later on.

Basting and sauces
Meat cooked on a rotisserie is self-basting so there is really no need to touch it during cooking, except perhaps to test it occasionally with a meat thermometer. For the barbecue recipes that do call for basting, simply place a foil tray on the coals to catch the meat's juices and then baste it in the usual way. Foil trays are available at most supermarkets, or they can be constructed by shaping a piece of double-thickness foil into the form of a shallow tray, using paper clips to secure the corners.

For applying sauces to meat, a pastry brush or clean small paint brush are the best things to use. If the sauce contains sugar, tomato ketchup or anything else

that burns easily, do not apply it until the final stage of the cooking. This not only saves the grill, but it also prevents the meat from tasting nasty on the outside.

When the cooking is over

In these energy-saving days, it is comforting to know that even charcoal can be saved and used again. You can salvage any charcoal that has not been burned by closing the vent in the barbecue and letting the fire die out. Simply extract any of the black coals, the ones that have not been burned, and add them to your fresh supply of charcoal, which should be kept in a dry place.

Dispose of the ashes in a rubbish bin or save them for a weed-killing agent in the garden, and wipe the barbecue to rid it of fat and grease. If it is a portable barbecue take it inside after the ashes have been disposed of, to prevent it from rusting.

Left: A plate-warmer and food storage rack make this an efficient barbecue.

A barbecue party

Long, balmy evenings and wide, starlit skies mark the arrival of summer to stay. Seize the moment and celebrate with a barbecue party; after all, the garden looks and smells its best at this time of year and because of this makes a lovely setting for entertaining.

Like any other party, a barbecue depends upon wise and thoughtful planning, so try to organize as much beforehand as possible. You will enjoy it so much more and so will your guests.

How many people?

Apart from the date, the number of people is a prime consideration for a barbecue. Common sense and your own purse or pocketbook usually determine the numbers, but all too frequently a zealous host or hostess tries to entertain too many people at once, with unfortunate results telling the tale. What you want to avoid is the claustrophobic situation of twenty or more people cramped into a small space with the last person to reach the barbecue itself being fed hours after the first and the barbecue chef approaching collapse after catering for so long and so many.

If space is a problem, keep the numbers low; a good party does not have to be large. Similarly, if your barbecue is small and cooks only a little at a time, don't have an enormous gathering.

Share-a-party

Perhaps you have a large barbecue with ample space and a friend who would also like to have a barbecue but lacks the facilities. If this is the case, and you are prepared to organize a joint party, then nothing is stopping you from inviting several guests. The only word of warning here is to have a party with someone whose friends will mix well with your own, lest you find yourself co-hostess of two opposing factions. Nothing is guaranteed to put a damper on an evening more than a 'Sharks and Jets' situation.

The great advantage about sharing a party is that it enables you to divide not only the costs but also the labour. About a week before the barbecue, and well after the invitations have gone out and the replies have come in, you and your friend should sit down and discuss the menu. Having decided what you want to feed the guests, make arrangements for shopping and food preparations. The easiest way to divide the shopping is course by course, not forgetting the drink and keeping a close record of costs, so that you can settle at the end. Having done the shopping, each of you should prepare and refrigerate as much as possible in advance. On the day of the party itself, invite your friend to your house where you can tackle the finishing touches together.

Easy to forget

Be sure, whether it is a joint party or your own, to get your figures right with regard to eating utensils. Decide whether to use paper and plastic utensils — an invaluable time-saver for the person washing up — or the real thing. If you do opt for the latter, you would be wise not to use your best bone china or crystal, as they break so easily and cost a fortune to replace.

Serving utensils and dishes should also be taken into consideration, especially if you are having a lavish, multi-course party. Think of what you will need in the way of dip, punch and salad bowls, serving dishes, sauce boats or jugs, bread boards and knives and butter dishes. If your personal supply does fall short of your requirements, which it may well do, borrow what you need from a friend or catering service. Do not forget ice and cork screws for the drinks table, for without them the party might as well not proceed.

Presentation of the food

How you actually arrange the food is your own decision, but if you are having a large party it makes sense to organize the food according to courses, i.e., one table for hors d'oeuvres and starters, one for bread, salads and meat sauces and one for dessert. Cover any food, if you think it's necessary, for unveiling the moment before serving. Cheese, for example, should be covered with a damp cloth and bread wrapped in foil. The dessert, if it's chilled, probably will not be brought to the table until just before serving, but there is no reason why you should not place the plates, cutlery and serving utensils on the dessert table before the guests arrive.

When laying out the tables there are three major things to bear in mind:

1. Place the food within easy reach of the guests.
2. Be sure that all of the relevant utensils, plates, bowls and napkins are there with each course.
3. Make them look as attractive as possible — a vase of flowers, a simple table cloth and a candle work wonders.

To capture the true barbecue spirit, arrange the food outdoors in the barbecue area — but not too close to the barbecue itself. In climates where insects are a problem, it makes more sense for people to help themselves to food indoors for taking it outside to eat; although if the weather is cold, you would be wise to make provisions for indoor-eating, in any case — similarly, if it rains.

When placing the tables, keep them well away from the barbecue to prevent the chef from being hemmed in by plate-loading guests. On the other hand, don't place the food tables so far away from the

barbecue that people have to walk a marathon. If you have garden chairs and tables, and the barbecue party is a small one, people can have a sit-down meal; otherwise, the guests can eat standing up. For the guests who really do find it awkward to eat standing up, provide a few chairs or small tables for plates and glasses.

A few disposal bins in unobtrusive corners (but not so unobtrusive that they can not be seen) never go amiss. They serve as a quiet reminder for people to lose their used paper plates and empty beer cans. Not everyone will oblige in your litter campaign, but this is to be expected and certainly not worried about.

Lighting

There is no point in going to a lot of trouble to provide appetizing food if no one can see it, so be sure to make adequate provisions for lighting at your night-time barbecues. Floodlights attached to the house are one form of electric lighting; a string of outdoor lights wrapped around strategically placed trees or poles is also effective. Otherwise, portable oil and gas lamps or even large candles throw a good light; if you use them, though, be sure they do not present a fire hazard.

Drinks

As a barbecue is focussed upon eating, the most sensible drinks to serve are wine and/or beer. Preferably, have red and white wine (half and half is a fair division), and keep the white chilled in an ice-filled container. As soon as your guests arrive offer them a drink and make it clear to them, assuming you do not wish to play bartender all evening, to help themselves.

If you are really feeling ambitious, have a punch at the start of the party. More potent than wine or beer, a punch provides just the right 'kick' to break the early-evening ice.

For the non-alcoholic drinkers, be sure to have plenty of soft beverages on hand. Again, an ice-filled bucket is a must and there are recipes in the next chapter for punches of both this and the alcoholic kind.

After-dinner coffee

By the time the coffee is ready to be served, your guests will have been outside for several hours and they could well be in need of a change. Rather than serve the coffee outside, therefore, why not urge your guests to come inside for it? The option is then open for them to stay inside if they would prefer it.

Ice breakers

Start off your barbecue with a bang, or more specifically with a fruity, thirst-slaking punch. Whether it's a Spanish sangria that captures your imagination, a tropical pineapple punch or a non-alcoholic citrus tea cup, you will find recipes for them all, and more, in this chapter. When you run out of punch, move on to wine, beer or a soft beverage.

Below: Beer and wine are always welcome drinks.

Potent for a start

Jamaican rum punch
ABOUT 24 SERVINGS
125 g / 4 oz sugar
600 ml / 1 pint strong tea, warm
225 ml / 8 fl oz fresh lemon juice
225 ml / 8 fl oz fresh orange juice
600 ml / 1 pint gin
900 ml / 1½ pints Jamaican rum
1.2 L / 2 pints ginger ale, chilled
4 mint sprigs, washed
125 g / 4 oz cherries, washed and stoned

Place the sugar in a large mixing bowl. Pour in the warm tea and stir until the sugar has dissolved.

Place the bowl in the refrigerator and chill for 30 minutes, or until the tea is cold.

Remove the bowl from the refrigerator and add the lemon juice, orange juice, gin, rum and ginger ale and stir well.

Place some ice cubes in a punch bowl and pour the punch over them. Garnish the punch with the mint and cherries and serve at once.

Fish House punch
ABOUT 32 SERVINGS
700 ml / 24 fl oz clear lemon juice
350 g / 12 oz brown sugar
2 standard-sized bottles Jamaican rum
1 bottle brandy
2 L / 3 pints cold water
175 ml / 6 fl oz peach bitters
275 g / 10 oz fresh and peeled, or

10

canned and drained, sliced peaches, roughly chopped

Place the lemon juice and sugar in a large punch bowl. Stir well to dissolve the sugar. Add the rum, brandy, water, bitters and peaches. Stir well to combine the ingredients.

Leave the punch for at least 3 hours, stirring occasionally.

Put a large block of ice in the bowl and serve in glasses or punch cups.

Pineapple punch
8–12 SERVINGS
600 ml / 1 pint pineapple juice
300 ml / 10 fl oz orange juice
½ bottle dry white wine
45–60 ml / 3–4 tbs brandy
Soda water
Grapes
Sliced mixed fruit of your choice

Pour the fruit juices, wine and brandy into a large jug. Mix and chill well.

Add soda water to taste just before serving.

Garnish with grapes and slices of other fruits.

Sparkling white wine cup
10–12 SERVINGS
12 ice-cubes
1 ice-cold bottle of sparkling white wine
50 ml / 2 fl oz Curacao
175 ml / 6 fl oz brandy
600 ml / 1 pint orange juice
600 ml / 1 pint ice-cold soda water

Put the ice-cubes in a large jug and add all the ingredients.

Stir well and served immediately.

Sangria
ABOUT 8 SERVINGS
1 bottle Spanish red wine
600 ml / 1 pint lemonade
60 ml / 4 tbs brandy
1 orange, sliced
2 limes, sliced
2 lemons, sliced
2–3 cloves
20–24 ice cubes

Pour the wine, lemonade and brandy into a jug. Add slices of orange, lime, and lemon, the cloves and ice cubes. Stir and serve immediately.

Temperance brews

California cocktail
6–8 SERVINGS
300 ml / 10 fl oz orange juice
300 ml / 10 fl oz apple juice
300 ml / 10 fl oz grape juice
Juice of 1 grapefruit
Juice of 2 lemons
45–60 ml / 3–4 tbs crushed ice
30 ml / 2 tbs sultanas or raisins
1 red dessert apple, cored and sliced
Soda water

Pour all the juices into a large pitcher and add the ice, sultanas or raisins and slices of apple.

Stir well and pour into glasses.

Add a dash of soda water just before serving.

Citrus tea cup
6 SERVINGS
900 ml / 1½ pints freshly made China tea
Thinly pared zest of 1 orange
1 thinly sliced lemon
1 clove
6 mm / ¼ in thick cinnamon stick
10 ml / 2 tsp rose-water (optional)

Heat together all the ingredients until hot but not boiling.

Set aside to cool and infuse. Strain. Reheat when required and add honey and sugar to taste.

Serve in tall heat-proof glasses with a slice of orange or lemon.

Right: Cool and refreshing, pineapple punch is a real thirst quencher.

While they wait

The smell of burning charcoal alone is enough to get most peoples' appetites going, so be sure to provide a light starter while the chef readies the fire. Dips are super at a barbecue, because not only are they simple to prepare but they can be eaten so casually. For something to scoop them with, try one of our attractive crudité ideas. Or perhaps a summer soup appeals, in which case there are all sorts of chilled ones to choose from, including gazpacho, Vichyssoise and a very special mixed fruit soup. For colder days, try our warming watercress soup. If hors d'oeuvres sound more alluring, you will find delicious recipes for these in the final section of this chapter.

Below: A tempting selection of appetizers.

Dips and crudité

Garlic dip
SERVES 6–8
175 g / 6 oz unsalted cream cheese
2 garlic cloves, crushed
15 ml / 1 tbs double cream
5 ml / 1 tsp salt
2.5 ml / ½ tsp black pepper
2.5 ml / ½ tsp paprika

In a medium-sized mixing bowl combine all the ingredients except the paprika, beating them with a wooden spoon until a smooth paste is formed. Spoon the dip into a shallow serving bowl and sprinkle the paprika on top. Place the bowl in the refrigerator to chill before serving.

Pineapple and cream cheese dip
SERVES 4–6
175 g / 6 oz canned pineapple
125 g / 4 oz cream cheese
30 ml / 2 tbs tomato chutney or relish
60 ml / 4 tbs mayonnaise

Drain the pineapple and mash with a fork. Mix the cream cheese with the remaining ingredients and add the mashed pineapple. Chill and serve with small biscuits.

Cream cheese dip with rosemary
SERVES 6
175 g / 6 oz cream cheese
2.5 ml / ½ tsp powdered rosemary
250 ml / 8 fl oz mayonnaise
Salt and pepper

Mix the cream cheese well with the powdered rosemary and add the mayonnaise. Taste, and add the salt and pepper. This dip is delicious sandwiched between two small cream crackers.

Devilled dip
SERVES 10–12
50 g / 2 oz butter
1 small onion, finely chopped
50 g / 2 oz flour
600 ml / 1 pint milk
2.5 ml / ½ tsp cayenne pepper
2.5 ml / ½ tsp mild chilli powder
15 ml / 1 tbs wine vinegar
5 ml / 1 tsp prepared mustard
2.5 ml / ½ tsp salt
1.25 ml / ¼ tsp black pepper
5 ml / 1 tsp Worcestershire sauce
300 ml / 10 fl oz double cream, stiffly whipped

In a medium-sized saucepan, melt the butter over moderate heat. Add the onion and fry for 2–3 minutes. With a wooden spoon stir in the flour.

Remove the pan from the heat and gradually stir in the milk. Return the pan to the heat and bring the sauce to the boil, stirring constantly.

Reduce the heat to low. Add the cayenne pepper, chilli powder, vinegar, mustard, salt, pepper and Worcestershire sauce. Cook for 2–3 minutes, stirring constantly, or until the sauce is smooth and thick.

Remove the pan from the heat and pour the sauce into a serving bowl. When the sauce has cooled to room temperature, place the bowl in the refrigerator and leave to chill.

Just before serving, fold in the cream.

Guacamole
SERVES 10–12
3 medium-sized ripe avocados
15 ml / 1 tbs lemon juice
10 ml / 2 tsp olive oil
2.5 ml / ½ tsp salt
2.5 ml / ½ tsp black pepper
2.5 ml / ½ tsp ground coriander
1 hard-boiled egg, finely chopped
½ small green pepper, white pith removed, seeded and chopped
1½ chillis, blanched and chopped
2 spring onions, chopped
1 tomato, blanched, peeled, seeded and chopped

With a sharp knife, halve the avocados. Slice off the skins and cut out the stones, discarding both. Place the flesh in a medium-sized mixing bowl and mash it with a kitchen fork.

Add the lemon juice, olive oil, salt, pepper and coriander, and stir to blend. Still stirring, add the finely chopped egg, green pepper, chillis, spring onions and chopped tomato. The dip should be fairly thick. It is best used immediately, but if it is to be kept, cover the bowl with foil and store in the refrigerator.

Stir well before serving.

Taramasalata
SERVES 6
450 g / 1 lb smoked cod's roe, skinned
4 slices white bread, crusts removed
and soaked in milk for 15 minutes
4 garlic cloves, crushed
300 ml / 10 fl oz olive oil
60 ml / 4 tbs lemon juice
2.5 ml / ½ tsp freshly ground black pepper
¼ cucumber, thinly sliced
6 firm tomatoes, sliced
6 black olives

Place the cod's roe in a large mixing bowl and pound it with the end of a rolling pin, or use a pestle and mortar, until the gritty texture is eliminated.

Squeeze as much moisture out of the bread as possible and add it to the bowl, with the garlic. Continue pounding until the mixture is smooth.

Add the oil, a few drops at a time, pounding constantly and adding a little of the lemon juice from time to time. Continue pounding until the mixture forms a soft, smooth paste and is pale pink in colour.

Alternatively, place all the ingredients in the jar of an electric blender and blend at moderately high speed until a soft paste is formed.

Beat the pepper into the mixture and place it on a serving dish. Surround the paste with the cucumber and tomato slices and place olives on top. Serve with hot pita or toast.

Les crudités
SERVES 4
4 large, firm tomatoes
½ small cucumber
60 ml / 4 tbs French dressing
15 ml / 1 tbs chopped parsley
4 medium-sized carrots
1 shallot
90 ml / 6 tbs tarragon dressing*
8 stalks of celery
1 head chicory
15 ml / 1 tbs lemon juice
15 ml / 1 tbs olive oil

Thinly slice the tomatoes and cucumber and arrange them in small separate dishes. Sprinkle with French dressing and chopped parsley.

Peel and grate the carrots and shallot

and mix them with a little tarragon dressing. Arrange this in another dish. Cut the celery and the chicory into fine strips and dress with lemon juice and olive oil. Arrange them in a serving dish. If preferred all the vegetables can be placed together in a large bowl, and the sauces served separately.

The vegetables are often served with mayonnaise. They may also be served with sardines, tuna fish or artichoke hearts and a slice of ham, pâté or salami.

Tarragon dressing is made in the same way as French dressing, except that tarragon vinegar is used instead of plain wine vinegar.

Crudites avec aioli
SERVES 6
175 ml / 6 fl oz aioli sauce (garlic mayonnaise)
30 ml / 2 tbs chopped fresh parsley
4 celery stalks, thinly sliced
1 fennel, peeled and thinly sliced
4 carrots, scraped and sliced matchstick-thin
1 small cauliflower, washed and broken into small florets

1 green pepper, white pith removed, seeded and cut into thin strips

In a small serving bowl, combine the aioli sauce and the parsley. Place the bowl in the refrigerator and chill the sauce for 2 hours.

Arrange the vegetables decoratively, either on separate serving dishes or on one large serving dish.

Remove the sauce from the refrigerator and serve it with the vegetables.

Below: Fresh vegetables, attractively presented signify a good crudité.

14

Soups and morsels

Vichyssoise
SERVES 6
125 g / 4 oz butter
1 kg / 2 lb leeks, washed, trimmed and chopped
½ kg / 1 lb potatoes, peeled and chopped
2 celery stalks, trimmed and chopped

600 ml / 1 pint milk
5 ml / 1 tsp salt
2.5 ml / ½ tsp black pepper
2.5 ml / ½ tsp sugar
1.25 ml / ¼ tsp grated nutmeg
300 ml / 10 fl oz double cream
1.25 ml / ¼ tsp curry powder

In a large saucepan, melt the butter over moderate heat. When the foam subsides, add the leeks, potatoes and celery and fry, stirring constantly, for 8 minutes. Pour in the stock and milk and bring the mixture to the boil. Season the mixture with the salt, pepper, sugar and nutmeg.

Above: For perfect vichyssoise, sprinkle freshly chopped chives on top.

Reduce the heat to low, cover the pan and simmer the mixture, stirring occasionally, for 30–40 minutes or until the vegetables are soft.

Remove the pan from the heat and pour the mixture through a fine strainer into a large mixing bowl. Using the back of a wooden spoon, rub the vegetables through the strainer until only a dry pulp remains. Alternatively, you can purée the ingredients in an electric blender.

Stir half of the cream into the purée and set aside to cool. Place the bowl in the

15

refrigerator to chill for at least 4 hours before serving.

To serve, remove the bowl from the refrigerator. Spoon the soup into individual soup bowls and pour a little of the remaining cream into each bowl. Sprinkle a little curry powder over the soup and serve immediately.

Cucumber and mint soup

SERVES 4

1 small onion, chopped
900 ml / 1½ pints chicken stock
or water
1 cucumber
3 sprigs mint
7.5 ml / 1½ tsp cornflour
Salt and freshly ground black pepper
to taste
Green food colouring (optional)

Simmer the onion in the stock or water for 10 minutes or until soft. Peel and roughly chop the cucumber, reserving a little for the garnish. Add to the stock with 1 sprig of mint and simmer for 7

minutes. Put through a sieve or electric blender and return to the pan. Add a little cold water to the cornflour, mix well, and add to the soup. Boil the soup for 1 minute, stirring continuously. Season well.

Chill in the refrigerator. Add a little artificial food colouring if necessary. Garnish with very finely diced cucumber and the 2 remaining sprigs of mint, shredded.

Gazpacho

SERVES 4

3 slices of brown bread, cut into
2.5 cm / 1 in cubes
300 ml / 10 fl oz canned
tomato juice
2 garlic cloves, finely chopped
½ cucumber, peeled and finely
chopped
1 green pepper, white pith removed,
seeded and finely chopped
1 red pepper, white pith removed,
seeded and finely chopped
1 large onion, finely chopped

675 g / 1½ lb tomatoes, blanched,
peeled, seeded and chopped
75 ml / 3 fl oz olive oil
30 ml / 2 tbs red wine vinegar
2.5 ml / ½ tsp salt
1.25 ml / ¼ tsp black pepper
1.25 ml / ¼ tsp dried marjoram
1.25 ml / ¼ tsp dried basil
4 ice cubes (optional)

Place the bread cubes in a medium-sized mixing bowl and pour over the tomato juice. Leave the bread cubes to soak for 5 minutes, then squeeze them to extract the excess juice. Transfer them to a large mixing bowl, reserving the tomato juice.

Add the garlic, cucumber, peppers, onion and tomatoes to the soaked bread cubes and stir to mix. Purée the ingredients by pounding them to a paste in a mortar with a pestle and then rubbing them through a strainer, or by putting them through a food mill. Stir in the

Right: Cucumber and mint soup.

Below: Gazpacho, a delicious treat.

16

reserved tomato juice. If you are using a blender, purée the vegetables and bread cubes with the reserved tomato juice.

Add the oil, vinegar, salt, pepper, marjoram and basil to the purée and stir well. The soup should be the consistency of single cream, so add more tomato juice if necessary.

Turn the soup into a deep serving bowl and place it in the refrigerator to chill for at least 1 hour. Just before serving, stir the soup well and drop in the ice cubes.

Watercress soup
SERVES 4

1.2 L / 2 pints milk
½ kg / lb potatoes, cooked and mashed
5 ml / 1 tsp salt
2 bunches watercress, washed, shaken dry and coarsely chopped
25 g / 1 oz butter
75 ml / 3 fl oz single cream
30 ml / 2 tbs chopped fresh parsley
2.5 ml / ½ tsp black pepper

Pour the milk into a large saucepan and bring it to the boil over moderate heat. Add the potatoes and salt and stir with a wooden spoon until the mixture is well blended. Stir in the watercress and cook for 5 minutes. Remove the pan from the heat and stir in the butter and cream.

Pour the soup into a warmed soup tureen. Sprinkle over the parsley and pepper and serve at once.

Midsummer soup
SERVES 4

225 g / 8 oz full fat curd cheese
300 ml / 10 fl oz beef consommé
50 ml / 2 fl oz Madeira
60 ml / 4 tbs chopped fresh chives
2.5 ml / ½ tsp black pepper

Place a large strainer over a large mixing bowl. Using the back of a wooden spoon rub the cheese through the strainer. Gradually add the consommé, stirring it into the cheese with a wooden spoon to make a smooth mixture. When all the consommé has been incorporated and the mixture resembles thin cream, stir in the Madeira. Stir in the chives and the pepper.

Pour the soup into individual bowls. Place the bowls in the refrigerator and chill the soup for 2 hours before serving.

Iced fruit soup
SERVES 4

1 kg / 2 lb mixed fruit, washed, peeled and chopped
50 g / 2 oz sugar
Pinch salt
1 clove
1 × 5 cm / 2 in cinnamon stick
Juice and grated rind of 1 lemon
1.2 L / 2 pints water

Place the fruit in a large saucepan. Add the sugar, salt, clove, cinnamon stick, lemon juice and rind. Pour in the water and bring the mixture to the boil over high heat, stirring occasionally. Reduce the heat to low, cover the pan and cook the fruit for 10–15 minutes, or until it is tender but still firm. Remove and discard the cinnamon stick.

Strain the contents of the pan into a large serving bowl, rubbing the fruit through the strainer with the back of a wooden spoon. Discard any pulp remaining in the strainer. Set the soup aside to cool for 15 minutes. Then place the soup in the refrigerator to chill for at least 1 hour before serving. Serve with whipped or sour cream, if desired.

Below: Fruit soup, an appetizing change.

18

Mexican stuffed eggs
SERVES 6
6 hard-boiled eggs
1 medium-sized avocado, peeled,
stoned and flesh chopped
1 small onion, finely minced
1 small green pepper, white pith
removed, seeded and finely minced
125 g / 4 oz prawns or shrimps,
shelled, deveined and finely chopped
5 ml / 1 tsp lemon juice
5 ml / 1 tsp wine vinegar
2.5 ml / ½ tsp salt
2.5 ml / ½ tsp black pepper
Pinch cayenne pepper
15 ml / 1 tbs chopped fresh parsley

Slice the eggs in half, lengthwise, and
scoop out the yolks. Set the egg whites
aside. Using the back of a wooden spoon
rub the yolks and the avocado flesh
through a fine nylon strainer into a
medium-sized mixing bowl. Stir in the
onion, green pepper and chopped prawns
or shrimps.

Add the lemon juice, vinegar, salt,
pepper and cayenne, mixing well to
blend. With a teaspoon, generously stuff
the egg white halves with the mixture.
Arrange the stuffed eggs on a serving
dish.

Sprinkle with the parsley and chill the
eggs, covered, in the refrigerator for at
least 30 minutes before serving. Serve on
a bed of lettuce leaves, garnished with
sliced tomatoes and olives.

Above: Mexican stuffed eggs.   *Below:* Marinated mushrooms.

Marinated mushrooms
SERVES 6–8
½ kg / 1 lb small button mushrooms,
stalks removed and wiped clean
Marinade:
5 ml / 1 tsp salt
3 black peppercorns, coarsely
crushed
10 ml / 2 tsp finely chopped fresh dill
or 5 ml / 1 tsp dried dill
60 ml / 4 tbs tarragon vinegar
15 ml / 1 tbs fresh lemon juice
50 ml / 2 fl oz olive oil

In a medium-sized, shallow mixing bowl,
combine the marinade ingredients
thoroughly.

Add the mushrooms and stir to coat
them with the liquid.

Cover the dish and set it aside to
marinate in a cool place for 2 hours,
basting the mushrooms frequently with
the marinade.

Drain off and discard the marinade
and pile the mushrooms in a serving dish.
Serve immediately.

19

On the coals

What will you have? Sweet and sour spare-ribs? Rotisseried duck? Or perhaps fresh trout wrapped in a parcel of foil? There is such a varied selection of fare in this chapter that you could barbecue virtually a different dish every night of the summer. For the steak and hamburger fans, we have several recipes for you as well — really tempting ones. To get the perfect fire, skim through the opening pages where you will find excellent hints on barbecue techniques.

Below: Just a few of the foods you can barbecue.

Quick but delicious

Ham steaks with barbecue sauce
SERVES 4
15 ml / 1 tbs butter
4 ham or gammon steaks, 4 cm
/ 1½ in thick, trimmed of fat
225 ml / 8 fl oz hot barbecue
sauce (last section of chapter)

Using a pastry brush, brush a little melted butter over the ham steaks.

When the fire is ready, lay the ham steaks on the barbecue and cook for 3–5 minutes on each side.

Serve with the barbecue sauce.

When preparing ham steaks (above), snip edges to prevent curling.

Barbecued pork chops
SERVES 6
6 loin pork chops, about 2.5 cm
/ 1 in thick
Salt and pepper
Sauce:
50 ml / 2 fl oz red wine vinegar
125 ml / 4 fl oz tomato ketchup
10 ml / 2 tsp sugar
2.5 ml / ½ tsp ground cloves
5 ml / 1 tsp celery seeds
2.5 ml / ½ tsp dry mustard
1 bay leaf

In a medium-sized mixing bowl, combine all of the sauce ingredients, mixing well to blend. Place in a saucepan and simmer the mixture for at least 30 minutes, to allow the flavours to combine.

Rub the pork chops all over with salt and pepper and keep them in a cool place until it is time to cook them.

When the fire is ready, place the chops on the barbecue rack and cook for 2–3 minutes on each side, or until each side is well browned. Then cook for a further 7 minutes on each side.

For convenience you can heat the sauce by the fire just before serving and let each guest spoon their own onto their chop. Alternatively, the sauce may be served cold.

Pork steaks with gherkins and mushroom sauce
SERVES 8
4 pork fillets
4 large sweet pickled gherkins
Salt and pepper

Sauce:
25 g / 1 oz butter
225 g / 8 oz button mushrooms,
wiped clean and thinly sliced
125 ml / 4 fl oz stock
300 ml / 10 fl oz double
cream
15 ml / 1 tbs soy sauce
2.5 ml / ½ tsp salt
30 ml / 2 tbs dry sherry

Melt the butter in a saucepan and sauté the mushrooms for a few minutes. Add all the remaining ingredients and cook gently for 3–4 minutes on a low heat, stirring frequently to prevent the cream from curdling. Set aside and keep warm.

Cut the pork fillets in half, removing sinews and surplus fat. Beat the meat flat with a meat hammer.

Slice the gherkins into 4 slices, lengthwise.

When the fire is ready, place the meat on the barbecue and cook for 5–7 minutes on each side. Cook the gherkins for 3–4 minutes on each side, by placing them on foil on the barbecue. When the meat is ready to serve, dish it up and place 2 gherkin slices on top. Reheat the sauce, and spoon it over the gherkins and chops. Serve immediately.

Hamburgers with herbs
SERVES 6

1½ kg / 3 lb lean minced beef
50 g / 2 oz fresh breadcrumbs
5 ml / 1 tsp salt
2.5 ml / ½ tsp black pepper
2.5 ml / ½ tsp dried thyme
1 egg, lightly beaten
Accompaniments:
3 medium-sized tomatoes, thinly
sliced
1 large onion, thinly sliced and
pushed out into rings
6 large lettuce leaves
6 hamburger or large soft buns
50 g / 2 oz butter

In a medium-sized mixing bowl, combine the beef, breadcrumbs, salt, pepper, thyme and egg, using your hands to mix the ingredients together thoroughly.

Form the beef mixture into six balls and flatten them into patty shapes. Set aside, and refrigerate if necessary.

Arrange the tomato slices, onion rings and lettuce leaves on a large serving plate. Set aside.

Split the hamburger buns in half and butter each half.

Place the beef patties on the barbecue rack and cook for 2–3 minutes on each

side, or until the hamburgers are well-browned. Then cook for a further 5–7 minutes on each side or until they are done as you like them.

Just before you take the hamburgers off the fire, you can heat the rolls over it if the coals are not too hot. Otherwise put them into a cool oven at the time the 'chef' starts cooking the hamburgers.

When the hamburgers are cooked, place each one on a bun and serve immediately with the accompaniments.

Hamburgers with sherry
SERVES 4

675g / 1½ lb lean minced
beef
2 small carrots, scraped and grated
Pinch of dried oregano
2.5 ml ½ tsp sugar
Pinch of salt
1.25 ml / ¼ tsp black pepper
60 ml / 4 tbs sherry
3 spring onions, chopped
15 ml / 1 tbs finely chopped fresh
parsley
25 g / 1 oz fresh breadcrumbs
8 stuffed green olives, finely chopped
1 egg, lightly beaten
4 hamburger or large soft buns
25g / 1 oz butter
225 ml / 8 fl oz hot barbecue
sauce (last section of chapter)

In a large mixing bowl, mix together the beef, carrots, oregano, sugar, salt, pepper and sherry. Add the spring onions chopped, parsley, breadcrumbs, olives and egg. With your hands, mix the ingredients until they are thoroughly blended. Shape the mixture into four medium-sized balls, and flatten them into patty shapes. Set aside.

Split the hamburger buns in half and butter each half. Set aside.

Place the beef patties on the barbecue rack and cook each side for about 2–3 minutes, or until the hamburgers are well-browned. With a pastry brush or spoon spread a little of the barbecue sauce over the hamburgers. Continue to cook for a further 5–7 minutes on each side, or until the hamburgers are cooked as you and your guests like them, basting occasionally with the barbecue sauce.

Place a hamburger on one-half of each bun. Spoon the remaining barbecue sauce over each hamburger and cover with the bun tops. Serve immediately.

Right: *For simplicity and flavour, a hamburger is difficult to match at a barbecue. Try our interesting recipes.*

Barbecued chicken
SERVES 4

2 small chickens
60 ml / 4 tbs vegetable oil
Sauce:
30 ml / 2 tbs olive oil
30 ml / 2 tbs Worcestershire sauce
30 ml / 2 tbs tomato purée
1 small onion, finely chopped
45 ml / 3 tbs red wine
1 garlic clove, crushed
10 ml / 2 tsp paprika
2.5 ml / ½ tsp cayenne pepper
5 ml / 1 tsp salt
2.5 ml / ½ tsp black pepper
5 ml / 1 tsp brown sugar

Make the sauce as for the barbecue sauce recipe in the final section of this chapter, substituting the cayenne pepper and paprika for the ginger.

Split the chickens in half. Wash them under cold, running water and dry them thoroughly. Brush with the oil just before cooking.

When the fire is ready, place the chicken pieces on the barbecue, skin sides up to begin with. Turn the chicken after about 6 minutes and cook the other side for 6 minutes. When both sides are brown, brush the chicken with the sauce, cooking for another 20 minutes or so, turning and brushing with the sauce

occasionally. Reheat the remaining sauce and spoon over the barbecued chicken to serve.

If you feel it would be too messy to baste the chicken with the sauce, omit this process and heat the sauce to serve purely as an accompaniment.

Mixed grill
SERVES 4
4 medium-sized lamb chops
4 pork sausages
25 g / 1 oz butter
8 mushrooms, trimmed

4 tomatoes, halved
1 bunch watercress

Start the lamb chops and the sausages first, as these will take about 15 minutes to cook.

Wipe and trim the chops and place on the barbecue rack with the sausages, remembering to turn the sausages gradually as they brown. Seal the chops for 2 minutes on each side and then cook for a further 6–7 minutes each side.

Before the meat is finished cooking, place a frying pan on the barbecue. Melt the butter and fry the mushrooms whole and the tomatoes, cut side downward. Cook for about 3 minutes and serve with the meat, and a sprig of watercress.

If your barbecue does not have enough space to accommodate a frying pan, simply fry the vegetables in your kitchen.

Spareribs with sweet and sour sauce
SERVES 4
1½ kg / 3 lb spareribs of pork, cut into serving pieces
Sauce:
30 ml / 2 tbs vegetable oil
1 garlic clove, crushed
1 large onion, finely chopped
150 ml / 5 fl oz tomato purée
45 ml / 3 tbs lemon juice
2.5 ml / ½ tsp salt
1.25 ml / ¼ tsp black pepper
2.5 ml / ½ tsp dried sage
60 ml / 4 tbs light brown sugar
125 ml / 4 fl oz beef stock
60 ml / 4 tbs Worcestershire sauce
10 ml / 2 tsp dry mustard

To prepare the sauce, heat the oil in a large frying pan over moderate heat. When the oil is hot, add the garlic and onion and cook for 3 minutes, stirring frequently until the onion is translucent and soft, but not brown.

Add the remaining sauce ingredients to the mixture in the frying pan and stir well.

Simmer over low heat for 10 minutes, stirring frequently.

Place the spareribs in the frying pan, in batches, turning them over to coat well with the sauce, then transfer to the barbecue rack.

Cook over cooler coals for 20–25 minutes, or until the ribs are cooked through, basting frequently with the sweet and sour sauce.

Serve hot, with any remaining sauce.

Lamb patties are a traditional Greek dish.

Lamb patties, Greek-style

SERVES 4

1 kg / 2 lb minced lamb
1 small onion, finely chopped
5 ml / 1 tsp salt
2.5 ml / ½ tsp black pepper
2.5 ml / ½ tsp grated nutmeg

24

150 g / 5 oz pine nuts or
blanched almonds, roughly chopped

Combine all the ingredients together, mixing well with two forks or your hands, until the mixture is well blended. Form into 12 small patties. Set aside and keep

cool until time to cook.

When the fire is ready, place the patties on the barbecue rack and cook for 8 minutes on each side, sealing each side first. If the patties brown too quickly, throw a tiny amount of water on the fire to reduce the heat. Serve immediately.

Marinade delights

Marinated steak
SERVES 4
675 g / 1½ lb rump steak
50 g / 2 oz butter
Freshly ground pepper
Marinade:
3.75 ml / ¾ tsp dry mustard
7.5 ml / 1½ tsp vinegar
7.5 ml / 1½ tsp soy sauce
5 ml / 1 tsp freshly squeezed
lemon juice

Prepare the marinade. Blend together the mustard and vinegar. Add the soy sauce and lemon juice. Place the steak in a dish, sprinkle it with freshly ground pepper and add the marinade. Leave for about 10 minutes, although the steak can be left in the marinade for a few hours if more convenient. Turn the steak in the marinade at least once.

When the fire is ready, cook the steak. Seal each side for a minute and then cook a further 2–5 minutes per side, depending on how you like it. Cut the steak on a platter into equal-sized portions and serve immediately.

Marinated lamb chops
SERVES 8
8 large lamb chops
Marinade:
90 ml / 6 tbs cooking oil
10 ml / 2 tsp French mustard
Juice of 1 lemon
30 ml / 2 tbs soy sauce
2 cloves of garlic, crushed
Salt and pepper

Mix together the oil, mustard, lemon juice, soy sauce, garlic and seasoning. Put into a large, shallow dish and add the chops.

Leave the chops to marinate for at least 6 hours in a cool place — preferably for 24 hours — and turn them occasionally.

When the fire is ready, place the chops on the barbecue and cook for about 20 minutes, sealing each side first.

Serve with barbecue sauce, which you can reheat by the fire.

(Recipe for the sauce appears at the end of this chapter.)

Steak teriyaki
SERVES 4
1 kg / 2 lb fillet steak, cut into 6 mm / ¼ in slices
Marinade:
1 × 2.5 cm / 1 in piece root ginger, peeled and finely chopped
2 garlic cloves, crushed
4 spring onions, finely chopped
30 ml / 2 tbs soft brown sugar
225 ml / 8 fl oz soy sauce
100 ml / 4 fl oz sake or dry sherry
5 ml / 1 tsp salt
2.5 ml / ½ tsp black pepper

Combine the marinade ingredients in a large shallow dish. Place the steak slices in the mixture and set aside to marinate at room temperature for 2 hours, basting occasionally.

When the fire is ready, transfer the steak to the barbecue using a slotted spoon.

Using a pastry brush, brush the steak with the marinade and cook for 3 minutes. Turn the steak, brush with a little more of the marinade and cook for a further 3 minutes. (These are the times for rare steaks; for well-done steaks, double the time.)

Remove from the heat and serve immediately.

Chicken teriyaki
SERVES 6
6 chicken breasts, skinned
Marinade:
30 ml / 2 tbs clear honey
100 ml / 4 fl oz soy sauce
5 ml / 1 tsp salt
5 ml / 1 tsp black pepper
2.5 cm / 1 in piece fresh root ginger, peeled and finely chopped
1 garlic clove, crushed
100 ml / 4 fl oz dry white wine

In a frying pan heat the honey over low heat until it liquifies slightly. Remove the pan from the heat and add the remaining marinade ingredients. Mix well. Place the chicken breasts in the marinade and set aside to marinate for 2 hours, basting occasionally.

Cook over the barbecue for about 5–7 minutes on each side, or until cooked through. Baste frequently with the marinade during cooking.

Heat the remaining marinade and serve with the chicken.

Lamb chops with rosemary
SERVES 4
4 thick lamb chops
Marinade:
50 ml / 2 fl oz olive oil
30 ml / 2 tbs lemon juice
2.5 ml / ½ tsp salt
1.25 ml / ¼ tsp black pepper
10 ml / 2 tsp dried rosemary
1 garlic clove, crushed

Combine the marinade ingredients in a medium-sized, shallow mixing bowl. Place the lamb chops in the marinade and baste them well. Set the chops aside in a cool place and marinate them for 2 hours, basting frequently.

When the fire is ready, place the chops on the barbecue and cook for 2 minutes on each side. Let them cook for a further 8 minutes on each side, basting frequently with the marinade.

Remove the chops from the barbecue and place them on a plate. Serve immediately.

Marinated skirt or flank steak
SERVES 4
1 kg / 2 lb skirt or flank steak, well beaten
Marinade:
75 ml / 3 fl oz soy sauce
75 ml / 3 fl oz medium sherry
75 ml / 3 fl oz olive oil
1 garlic clove, crushed
5 ml / 1 tsp salt
2.5 ml / ½ tsp black pepper

Mix together in a large shallow dish the soy sauce, sherry, oil, garlic, salt and pepper. Place the steaks in the marinade and leave them to marinate for at least 8 hours or overnight.

When the fire is ready, remove the steaks from the marinade and place them on the barbecue. Cook for 3–4 minutes on each side (for rare steaks).

Remove them from the barbecue and serve at once.

Spatchcock of chicken
SERVES 2–4
1 × 1½ kg / 3 lb chicken
45 ml / 3 tbs lemon juice
2.5 ml / ½ tsp salt
40 g / 1½ oz melted butter

Cut the chicken along the back bone and force open until flat. Press two long metal skewers into the drumstick on one side, through the breast and out of the drumstick on the other side. This will hold the chicken in shape during cooking and can be used to turn it.

Sprinkle with lemon juice and salt and set aside for 1 hour. When the fire is ready, brush the chicken with melted butter and cook over the barbecue for about 15 minutes on the bony side and 15 minutes on the reverse. The exact time will depend on the intensity of heat from the fire.

Carve into serving pieces and serve.

Below: Lamb chops combine well with the delicate flavour of tarragon. In this recipe, the marinade is more important than the leaves placed on top.

Tarragon lamb chops

SERVES 4

4 lamb chops, cut from the saddle
2.5 ml / $\frac{1}{2}$ tsp salt
1.25 ml / $\frac{1}{4}$ tsp black pepper
60 ml / 4 tbs olive oil
15 ml / 1 tbs chopped fresh tarragon
4 tomatoes, halved

Sprinkle the chops with the salt and pepper and rub them in with your fingertips. Place the chops in a shallow dish. In a small mixing bowl, combine the oil and chopped tarragon. Sprinkle the oil mixture over the chops and set aside for 30 minutes.

When the fire is ready, place the chops on the barbecue. Seal the chops for 2 minutes on each side and cook for a further 10 minutes a side, or until the chops are cooked, brushing frequently with the oil marinade.

About 5 minutes before the chops are finished, cook the tomatoes by placing them on a sheet of foil on the barbecue.

Remove the chops and tomatoes and serve immediately.

Right: Marinated, wrapped in foil or grilled whole, barbecued fish is a taste experience not to be missed. There are several recipes here to tempt you.

Japanese sardines

SERVES 4

½ kg / 1 lb fresh sardines, washed
thoroughly in cold water and dried
Marinade:
100 ml / 4 fl oz soy sauce
50 ml / 2 fl oz vinegar
30 ml / 2 tbs lemon juice
1 × 2.5 cm / 1 in piece root ginger
peeled and chopped
2 garlic cloves, crushed
30 ml / 2 tbs olive oil

In a small mixing bowl, combine the
marinade ingredients, reserving a little oil.

Arrange the sardines in a shallow
baking dish and pour the soy sauce
marinade over them. Leave the sardines
in a cool place to marinate for 2 hours.

Remove the sardines from the
marinade. Discard the marinade and dry
the fish on kitchen paper towels.

Place the sardines on the barbecue rack
and brush them with the remaining oil.
Cook them for 3–5 minutes or longer,
depending on their size, turning once so
that they are brown on both sides.

Serve immediately.

Spare ribs of pork

SERVES 6–8

1½ kg / 3 lb spare ribs of pork
1 large onion, grated
45 ml / 3 tbs sesame oil or olive oil
75 ml / 3 fl oz soy sauce

Separate the ribs with a sharp knife.

Peel and grate the onion and place in
a large bowl with the oil and soy sauce.
Add the ribs a few at a time, turning them
over several times to coat them in the
marinade. Set aside to marinate for at
least 1 hour, turning frequently.

Cook the spare ribs over the barbecue
until brown and crisp. Brush them frequently with the marinade during cooking
and serve with a spicy sauce.

Cooked to a turn

Spicy lamb
SERVES 6

1 × 1½–2 kg / 3–4 lb leg of lamb,
boned, rolled and tied
1 large garlic clove, sliced
10 ml / 2 tsp prepared mustard
2.5 ml / ½ tsp ground ginger
5 ml / 1 tsp salt
2.5 ml / ½ tsp ground black pepper
30 ml / 2 tbs flour
Sauce:
60 ml / 4 tbs chutney
45 ml / 3 tbs Worcestershire sauce
30 ml / 2 tbs soy sauce
30 ml / 2 tbs tomato purée
30 ml / 2 tbs red wine
45 ml / 3 tbs melted butter
1.25 ml / ¼ tsp cayenne pepper
1 onion, finely chopped
5 ml / 1 tsp brown sugar

With a sharp, pointed knife make slits in
the meat and insert the slices of garlic. In
a small bowl mix together the prepared
mustard, ginger, salt and pepper. Rub the
mixture over the surface of the meat.
Coat the meat with flour. In another bowl
mix together the sauce ingredients.

Place the lamb on the rotisserie spit,
about 12.5 cm / 5 in from the heat and
turn on the rotisserie motor. Cook,
basting with the sauce from time to time,
for 2–2½ hours or until the lamb is
cooked through. To test, pierce the meaty
part of the leg with a skewer; the juices
that run out should be faintly rosy. If you
are using a meat thermometer, it should
register 67°C / 155°F. Remove the lamb
from the spit and carve it into slices.
Spoon over remaining sauce and serve.

Barbecued duck
SERVES 4

1 × 2¼ kg / 5 lb duck
5 ml / 1 tsp dry mustard
1.25 ml / ¼ tsp cayenne pepper
2.5 ml / ½ tsp freshly ground black
pepper
Sauce:
1 garlic clove, crushed
1.25 ml / ¼ tsp Tabasco sauce
30 ml / 2 tbs Worcestershire sauce
30 ml / 2 tbs tomato purée
60 ml / 4 tbs red wine
10 ml / 2 tsp paprika
Grated rind and juice of 1 orange
30 ml / 2 tbs lemon juice
5 ml / 1 tsp brown sugar
1.25 ml / ¼ tsp black pepper
2.5 ml / ½ tsp salt
5 ml / 1 tsp arrowroot mixed with
5 ml / 1 tsp water (optional)

Rub the duck with the mustard, cayenne
and black pepper. Prick the skin all over
with a fork. Place the duck on the
rotisserie spit and put it over the coals.
Put a shallow pan made of foil under the
duck to catch the dripping fat. This pan
will have to be emptied frequently.

Mix all the ingredients for the sauce,
except for the arrowroot mixed with
water, together in a small bowl.

Cook the duck for 20 minutes before
basting it with the sauce. Continue cooking for 1½–2 hours, basting occasionally
with the sauce, until the duck is cooked
through. To test, pierce the thigh with a
skewer; the juices should be clear.

The remaining sauce may be thickened
with the dissolved arrowroot. To do this,
put the sauce into a saucepan, stir in the
arrowroot and simmer for 2 minutes,
stirring constantly.

Remove the duck from the spit, carve
and pour over the sauce.

Leg of lamb with coriander and garlic
SERVES 6–8

1 × 2¾ kg / 6 lb leg of lamb, boned,
rolled and tied
6 garlic cloves
15 ml / 1 tbs crushed coriander seeds
5 ml / 1 tsp salt
2.5 ml / ½ tsp black pepper
125 g / 4 oz butter, melted

With the tip of a sharp knife, make six
incisions in the leg of lamb. Press the
garlic cloves and coriander into the
incisions. Rub lamb with salt and pepper.

Place the lamb on the rotisserie spit and
brush it all over with melted butter. Put
the lamb over the coals, about 12.5 cm
/ 5 in from the heat and turn on the
rotisserie motor. Cook, basting with
butter from time to time, for 2½–3 hours
or until the lamb is cooked through. To
test, pierce the meaty part of the leg
with a skewer; the juices that run out
should be faintly rosy. If you are using a
meat thermometer it should register
67°C / 155°F. Remove the lamb from the
spit and carve it into slices.

Even small barbecues have rotisseries.

28

Foil fare
Featuring fish

Trout parcels
SERVES 6

6 rainbow or blue trout
6 sprigs fresh thyme
75 g / 3 oz butter
3 lemons
Salt and pepper

Gut the trout and rinse well. Put a sprig of thyme and an equal portion of the butter inside each trout. Place each fish on a double-thickness square of foil and sprinkle with the juice of half a lemon and salt and pepper. Wrap the foil securely, taking care not to leave any openings.

When the fire is ready, place on the barbecue grill and cook for about 30 minutes, turning once.

N.B. As a variation, use chicken drumsticks with finely shredded green pepper, finely chopped onion, salt and pepper and 15 g / ½ oz of butter. Increase the cooking time to about 1 hour.

Fish steaks in foil
SERVES 4

4 large cod or haddock steaks, about
225 g / 8 oz each
5 ml / 1 tsp salt
Sauce:
50 g / 2 oz butter
225 ml / 8 fl oz red wine
Pinch of cayenne pepper
5 ml / 1 tsp prepared mustard
10 ml / 2 tsp chilli sauce
30 ml / 2 tbs lemon juice
5 ml / 1 tsp brown sugar
15 ml / 1 tbs capers
2.5 ml / ½ tsp salt

Melt half the butter in a saucepan over moderate heat. Add all the remaining sauce ingredients. Stir to mix and bring to the boil. Reduce the heat and simmer for 10 minutes. Set the sauce aside.

Place the fish on double-thickness pieces of foil, sprinkling each piece with salt and dotting with butter. Fold the foil around the fish to enclose completely. Put aside in a cool place before cooking.

When the fire is ready, place the fish packets on the barbecue and cook for 4–5 minutes on each side. To test if the fish is cooked, open the foil. The fish is cooked when the flakes separate easily with a fork. Reheat the sauce.

To serve, remove each fish steak from the foil and place on a plate. Spoon the sauce over the fish.

Scandinavian herrings
SERVES 4

15 g / ½ oz butter
4 large herrings, cleaned and gutted
1 small onion, finely chopped
125 g / 4 oz mushrooms, wiped clean and sliced
30 ml / 2 tbs lemon juice
30 ml / 2 tbs chopped fresh parsley
5 ml / 1 tsp salt
2.5 ml / ½ tsp freshly ground black pepper
5 ml / 1 tsp dried dill

Cut out 4 pieces of foil large enough to enclose completely each fish, when the foil is folded in half. With the butter, grease each piece of foil.

Place each herring in the centre of a piece of double-thickness foil. Sprinkle the onion, mushrooms, lemon juice, parsley, salt, pepper and dill over each herring. Draw up the sides of the foil and fold the edges over to seal each herring completely. Place the fish parcels on the barbecue and bake for 25 or 30 minutes, turning the parcels occasionally. The fish is ready when the fish flakes easily when tested with a fork.

When cooked, serve immediately.

Left: These mackerel have been cooked in the same way as the trout parcels, with parsley being substituted for the thyme. Remember to wrap foil securely.

Featuring vegetables

Item to be barbecued	Single serving	Distance from heat	Cooking time
Potatoes scrubbed, pricked and wrapped in double-thickness foil	1 large	On the coals	1 hour
Corn-on-the-cob silk removed, shuck put back in place, buttered in double-thickness foil	1 ear	10 cm / 4 in	30–40 minutes
Frozen peas seasoned with sliced onion, chopped mint, salt, pepper and butter, wrapped in buttered foil	120 g / 4 oz	10 cm / 4 in	20–30 minutes
Courgettes sliced in half and covered with grated cheese, salt and pepper and wrapped in buttered foil	1 medium	7.5 cm / 3 in	20–30 minutes
Onions unpeeled, wrapped in double-thickness foil	1 medium	On the coals	1 hour

N.B. When roasting vegetables in foil, be sure that the dull side — not the shiny one — is exposed to the fire to reduce the risk of burning. The same applies to meat and fish which is cooked in foil.

Saucy meat toppings

Barbecue sauce
MAKES 225 ML / 8 FL OZ

25 g / 1 oz butter
1 onion, chopped
1 garlic clove, crushed
1.2 cm / ½ in piece fresh ginger,
peeled and finely chopped
150 ml / 5 fl oz water
400 g / 14 oz canned tomatoes
1 large celery stalk, chopped
30 ml / 2 tbs lemon juice
30 ml / 2 tbs vinegar
30 ml / 2 tbs tomato purée
22.5 ml / 4½ tsp Worcestershire sauce
10 ml / 2 tsp brown sugar
2.5 ml / ½ tsp dried oregano
1 large bay leaf
5 ml / 1 tsp salt
1.25 ml / ¼ tsp grated nutmeg

Melt the butter in a small saucepan over
moderate heat. Add the onion, garlic and
ginger and fry until the onion is soft and
translucent.

Add all the remaining ingredients,
cover and cook over low heat for 40
minutes. Strain the sauce, taste and add
more salt and sugar if necessary.

Chicken barbecue sauce
MAKES ABOUT 425 ML / 15 FL OZ

45 ml / 3 tbs cider vinegar
150 ml / 5 fl oz water
45 ml / 3 tbs sugar
30 ml / 2 tbs English mustard
2 garlic cloves, crushed
Freshly ground black pepper
5 ml / 1 tsp salt
1 medium-sized onion, finely
chopped
150 ml / 5 fl oz tomato
ketchup
Grated zest and juice of 1 lemon
15 ml / 1 tbs Worcestershire sauce
50 g / 2 oz butter

In a saucepan mix together all the
ingredients and heat until just below
boiling point. Do not boil. Simmer for
20 minutes. Serve immediately or reheat
before serving.

*Right: Fruit, vegetables and spices
combine to make a tremendous variety of
sauces for barbecued meat and fish.*

32

Herb and lemon sauce
MAKES ABOUT 300 ML / 10 FL OZ

15 g / ½ oz butter
1 garlic clove, crushed
15 ml / 1 tbs flour
300 ml / 10 fl oz milk
2.5 ml / ½ tsp dried thyme
15 ml / 1 tbs finely chopped fresh
chives
15 ml / 1 tbs finely chopped fresh
chervil
Finely grated rind of 1 lemon
1.25 ml / ¼ tsp salt
Pinch of black pepper
5 ml / 1 tsp lemon juice
15 ml / 1 tbs cream

In a medium-sized saucepan, melt the
butter over moderate heat. When the
foam subsides, add the garlic and cook,
stirring occasionally, for 4–5 minutes.

Remove the pan from the heat. With a
wooden spoon, stir in the flour to make a
smooth paste. Gradually add the milk,
stirring constantly. Stir in the thyme,
chives, chervil, lemon rind, salt and
pepper.

Return the pan to the heat and bring
the sauce to the boil, stirring constantly.
Reduce the heat to low, cover the pan
and simmer for 15 minutes, stirring
occasionally. Stir in the lemon juice and
cream and taste the sauce. Add more
seasoning if necessary.

Remove the pan from the heat and pour
the sauce into a warmed sauceboat. Serve
immediately.

This sauce is delicious with either fish
or chicken.

Tomato sauce
MAKES 750 ML / 1¼ PINTS

1½ kg / 3 lb tomatoes, halved
10 ml / 2 tsp salt
10 ml / 2 tsp sugar
5 ml / 1 tsp dried basil
2.5 ml / ½ tsp grated lemon rind

Preheat the oven to 170°C, 325°F, Gas
Mark 3.

Place the tomatoes in a large ovenproof
casserole. Cover the casserole with a well-
fitting lid or aluminium foil and place
in the oven. Bake the tomatoes for 45
minutes or until they are very soft.
Remove the casserole from the oven.

Place the tomatoes in a large strainer
over a large saucepan. Using the back of a
wooden spoon, rub the tomatoes through
the strainer until only a dry pulp is left.
Discard the pulp. Add the salt, sugar,
basil and lemon rind to the pan. Place the
pan over moderate heat and cook, stirring

frequently with the wooden spoon, for 10 minutes or until the mixture is fairly thick. Remove the pan from the heat.

Either pour the sauce into a warmed sauceboat and serve, or allow the sauce to cool completely. Pour it into a screw-top jar and refrigerate until required.

Mushroom ketchup
MAKES 900 ML / 1½ PINTS

1½ kg / 3 lb button mushrooms, wiped clean, trimmed and coarsely chopped
125 g / 4 oz salt
1 small onion, finely chopped
10 ml / 2 tsp pickling spices
6 black peppercorns, crushed
5 ml / 1 tsp ground mace
1.25 ml / ¼ tsp mixed spice or ground allspice
Juice of 2 lemons
75 ml / 3 fl oz brandy

Place a quarter of the mushrooms in a large ovenproof casserole and sprinkle with a quarter of the salt. Continue making layers of mushrooms and salt, ending with a layer of salt. Cover the casserole and set the mushrooms aside to dégorge for 24 hours, stirring occasionally.

Preheat the oven to 150°C, 300°F, Gas Mark 2.

Uncover the casserole and stir in the onion. Cover the casserole, place it in the oven and bake for 30 minutes. Remove the casserole from the oven.

Purée the mushrooms in a food mill or blender until the mixture is thick and smooth. Pour the purée into a medium-sized saucepan and add the pickling spices, peppercorns, mace, mixed spice (or allspice) and lemon juice. Set the pan over moderately high heat and, stirring constantly, bring slowly to the boil. Continue to boil for 3–5 minutes or until the purée has reduced slightly.

Remove the pan from the heat and set aside to cool completely. When the mixture is cold, stir in the brandy.

The ketchup is now ready to be used or stored in airtight bottles.

Kheera ka raita (Yogurt sauce)
SERVES 4–6

600 ml / 1 pint yogurt
½ cucumber, washed, diced and dégorged
4 spring onions, trimmed and finely chopped
2.5 ml / ½ tsp salt
2.5 ml / ½ tsp black pepper
1 green chilli, finely chopped
1.25 ml / ¼ tsp paprika

Above: Yogurt sauce with cucumber or mango, superb with barbecued meat.

In a medium-sized mixing bowl, beat the yogurt until it is smooth. Mix in the cucumber, spring onions, salt and pepper.

Pour the yogurt mixture into a serving bowl. Cover the bowl with plastic wrap and place it in the refrigerator for 1 hour or until it is thoroughly chilled.

Remove the bowl from the refrigerator and remove and discard the plastic wrap. Sprinkle the top with the chilli and paprika and serve immediately.

N.B. This sauce goes very well with highly spiced meats. If preferred, the chilli may be omitted.

34

Raita with mangoes (Yogurt and mango sauce)

SERVES 4–6
600 ml / 1 pint yogurt
2 ripe fresh mangoes, peeled, stoned and diced
2.5 ml / ½ tsp salt
15 ml / 1 tbs ghee or clarified butter
5 ml / 1 tsp mustard seed
1 green chilli, finely chopped
10 ml / 2 tsp finely chopped fresh coriander leaves

In a medium-sized mixing bowl, beat the yogurt until it is smooth. Mix in the mangoes and the salt.

Set aside.

In a small frying-pan, melt the ghee or clarified butter over moderate heat.

When it is hot, add the mustard seed and fry until the seeds begin to pop. Add the chilli and stir constantly for 10 seconds. Remove the pan from the heat. Tip the contents of the pan into the yogurt mixture. Stir well to mix. Pour the yogurt mixture into a serving bowl. Cover the bowl with plastic wrap and place it in the refrigerator for 1 hour or until it is thoroughly chilled.

Remove the bowl from the refrigerator and remove and discard the plastic wrap. Sprinkle the top with the coriander leaves and serve immediately.

N.B. Canned mangoes may be substituted if fresh ones are not available. This raita is also delicious made with guavas, rather than mangoes.

Stuck on kebabs

The mere mention of a kebab often conjures up exotic visions of Asia and the Middle East. In fact, a kebab is nothing more than cubes of meat or fish, and frequently chopped vegetables, cooked on metal skewers over an open fire — none of which require an overseas visit to obtain. You can have kebabs in the seclusion of your backyard or garden. The beauty of kebabs is how economical they are:

only a small amount of meat is used for the average serving and the rest is made up in vegetables. Of course they require some organization beforehand, but only a short time chopping up the ingredients and sticking them on skewers, and the results are worth every minute.

Below: Kebabs for colour at a barbecue.

Lamb kebabs in herb marinade
SERVES 6–8

1½ kg / 3 lb boned leg of lamb, cut
into 2.5 cm / 1 in cubes
225 ml / 8 fl oz olive oil
125 ml / 4 fl oz dry white wine
1 medium-sized onion, finely
chopped
1 celery stalk, finely chopped
1 garlic clove, crushed
5 ml / 1 tsp dried thyme
5 ml / 1 tsp dried basil
15 ml / 1 tbs chopped fresh chives
6 black peppercorns, crushed
1 bay leaf
5 ml / 1 tsp salt
350 g / 12 oz button mushrooms,
wiped clean
18 small whole tomatoes
8 small onions, peeled, boiled for 8
minutes and drained
50 g / 2 oz butter, melted

In a large shallow dish, combine the oil
and white wine. Add the chopped onion,
celery and garlic. Stir in the thyme, basil,
chives, peppercorns, bay leaf and salt.

Lay the meat cubes in the mixture and
leave to marinate for 6–8 hours at room
temperature, turning occasionally.

With a slotted spoon, lift the meat cubes
from the marinade and thread them on to
10 metal skewers, alternating with mushrooms, tomatoes and onions.

Pour the marinade through a strainer
into a large jug. Discard the vegetables
remaining in the strainer. Reserve the
marinade.

Using a pastry brush, coat the kebabs
with the melted butter. Place them on the
barbecue and cook for 2 minutes. Raise
the grill rack and continue cooking them
for a further 10–12 minutes, turning the
skewers once or twice and basting
occasionally with the reserved marinade.

Slide the meat and vegetables off the
skewers on to a serving dish and serve.

Shashlik
SERVES 4

1 kg / 2 lb lean loin of lamb, boned,
excess fat removed and cut into
2.5 cm / 1 in pieces
1 lemon, cut into wedges
Marinade:
75 ml / 3 fl oz vegetable oil
Juice of 1 large lemon
2 medium-sized onions, sliced
2.5 ml / ½ tsp salt
2.5 ml / ½ tsp black pepper

Combine in a large, shallow dish the oil,
lemon juice, onions, salt and pepper. Lay
36

the meat cubes in the mixture, cover and
place the dish in the refrigerator. Leave
to marinate for at least 8 hours or overnight, turning the meat occasionally.

Remove the dish from the refrigerator
and remove the cover.

With a slotted spoon, lift the meat
cubes from the marinade and thread them
on to 8 metal skewers, alternating with
tomato quarters and pieces of green
pepper. Set aside.

Pour the marinade through a strainer
into a large jug. Discard the contents of
the strainer.

Using a pastry brush, coat the meat,
tomatoes and peppers with the strained
marinade. Place the skewers on the
barbecue and cook for 4 minutes, turning
once.

Continue cooking the kebabs for a
further 5–8 minutes, turning the skewers
and basting occasionally with the reserved
marinade.

Remove the kebabs from the heat and
serve immediately, garnished with lemon
wedges.

Portuguese kebabs
SERVES 4–6

½ kg / 1 lb pork fillets cut into
2.5 cm / 1 in cubes
½ kg / 1 lb boned shoulder of lamb, cut
into 2.5 cm / 1 in cubes
Marinade:
4 garlic cloves, crushed
15 ml / 1 tbs paprika
5 ml / 1 tsp dried oregano
10 ml / 2 tsp grated orange rind
5 ml / 1 tsp salt
2.5 ml / ½ tsp black pepper
5 ml / 1 tsp sugar
15 ml / 1 tbs finely chopped fresh
mint
15 ml / 1 tbs olive oil
30 ml / 2 tbs dry sherry

First prepare the marinade. In a medium-
sized mixing bowl, combine the garlic,
paprika, oregano, orange rind, salt,
pepper, sugar, mint, oil and sherry
together. With a kitchen fork, beat the
ingredients until they are thoroughly
combined. Add the meat pieces and baste
them thoroughly with the marinade. Set
aside to marinate for 2 hours, basting
occasionally.

With a slotted spoon, lift the meat
cubes from the marinade and thread them
on metal skewers, alternating the pork
and lamb. Reserve the marinade.

Place the skewers on the barbecue and,
using a pastry brush, brush the meat
with the marinade. Cook the meat for

10–15 minutes, turning the skewers two
or three times and basting occasionally
with the remaining marinade.

Slide the meat off the skewers on to a
serving dish and serve immediately.

Greek lamb kebabs
SERVES 6

1 kg / 2 lb shoulder of lamb, boned
and cut into 2.5 cm / 1 in cubes
4 onions
Marinade:
Juice of 2 lemons
120 ml / 8 tbs olive oil
2.5 ml / ½ tsp salt
5 ml / 1 tsp black pepper
2.5 ml / ½ tsp dried marjoram

For the marinade, mix together in a large
shallow bowl the lemon juice, oil, salt,
pepper and marjoram. Put the meat into
the bowl and using a spoon, turn the
meat over until it is coated with the
marinade. Cover and set aside to
marinate for 1 hour.

Cut the onions into quarters and
separate the layers. If the onions are large,
cut the quarters in half horizontally.

Thread the lamb on to metal skewers
alternately with the onion. Discard the
marinade.

Place the kebabs on the barbecue and
cook them for 14 minutes or until the
edges are dark brown, turning the skewers
occasionally.

Remove the kebabs from the barbecue
and serve immediately.

Tikka kebab
SERVES 4

1 kg / 2 lb boned leg of lamb, cut into
2.5 cm / 1 in cubes
5 ml / 1 tsp salt
25 g / 1 oz butter, melted
Marinade:
10 cm / 4 in piece fresh root ginger,
peeled and chopped
3 medium-sized onions, chopped
1 small bunch fresh coriander leaves,
washed and shaken dry
15 ml / 1 tbs whole coriander seeds
Juice of 1 lemon
2 green chillis
2.5 ml / ½ tsp black peppercorns

For the marinade, put the ginger, onions,
coriander leaves and seeds, lemon juice,
green chillis and peppercorns in the jar

*Right: Portuguese kebabs are made with
cubes of lamb and pork, soaked first in a
spicy marinade sauce.*

of an electric blender. Blend at high speed until the mixture forms a purée, adding a little more lemon juice if necessary.

Put the spice mixture into a large mixing bowl. Add the lamb cubes and mix well. Cover the bowl and set aside to marinate for at least 4 hours.

Thread the meat on to metal skewers and sprinkle over the salt and melted butter. Arrange the skewers over the barbecue. Cook for 8–10 minutes, turning the skewers occasionally, or until the lamb is cooked.

Remove from the heat. Slide the meat off the skewers on to a warmed serving dish and serve immediately.

Seekh kebabs
SERVES 4
2.5 ml / ½ tsp butter
700 g / 1½ lb finely minced meat
50 g / 2 oz fresh white breadcrumbs
1 × 2.5 cm / 1 in piece fresh root ginger, peeled and finely chopped or grated
1 green chilli, finely chopped
2 garlic cloves, crushed
5 ml / 1 tsp ground cumin
2.5 ml / ½ tsp salt
5 ml / 1 tsp finely grated lemon rind
5 ml / 1 tsp lemon juice

Lightly grease 8 thick skewers with the butter. Set aside.

In a medium-sized mixing bowl, combine all the remaining ingredients. Using your hands, mix and knead the ingredients together.

Divide the meat mixture into 16 equal portions. With wetted hands, press 8 portions on to the skewers into pencil shapes, gently pressing the meat mixture until the kebabs measure 10 cm / 4 in in length.

When the fire is ready, place the 8 skewers on the barbecue, and cook, turning the kebabs once, for 6 minutes or until the kebabs are cooked through and browned all over.

Serve the first batch while you finish cooking the remaining 8 kebabs.

Serve immediately.

Seekh Kebabs (seekh k'babs) are traditionally made with lamb but quality beef may be substituted if minced lamb is not available. In India and Pakistan the skewers are as thick as a pencil so that the meat can be thinly spread and cooked quickly under high heat. Serve the kebabs with nan or pita and an onion and tomato salad.

Below: *Minced meat, either lamb or beef, forms the basic ingredient of these seekh kebabs.*

Chicken tikka
SERVES 4– 6
3 whole chicken breasts, skinned and boned
Marinade:
150 ml / 5 fl oz yogurt
4 garlic cloves, crushed
2.5 cm / 1 in piece fresh root ginger, peeled and finely chopped or grated
1 small onion, grated
7.5 ml / 1½ tsp hot chilli powder
15 ml / 1 tbs ground coriander
5 ml / 1 tsp salt
Garnish:
1 large onion, thinly sliced and pushed out into rings
2 large tomatoes, thinly sliced
30 ml / 2 tbs chopped fresh coriander leaves

In a medium-sized mixing bowl, combine the yogurt, garlic, ginger, onion, chilli powder, coriander and salt, beating well to mix. Set aside.

Cut the chicken meat into 2.5 cm / 1 in cubes. Add the cubes to the marinade and mix well to coat. Cover the bowl and place it in the refrigerator. Leave to marinate for at least 6 hours or overnight.

Thread the chicken cubes on to skewers. Place the skewers on the barbecue and cook the chicken cubes, turning them occasionally, for 5–6 minutes or until they are cooked.

Above: Chicken with orange and figs is a delightful combination of flavours.

Remove the skewers from the heat. Slide the kebabs off the skewers on to a warmed serving dish. Garnish with the onion rings, sliced tomatoes and chopped coriander leaves. Serve immediately with chappati, nan or pita.

Chicken with orange and figs
SERVES 8
50 g / 2 oz butter
16 chicken portions
3 large oranges
16 fresh or dried figs
400 ml / 15 fl oz chicken barbecue sauce (see preceding chapter)

Melt the butter in a large frying pan and sauté the chicken portions for 5–6 minutes. This cuts down the barbecue time.

Cut each orange into 6 segments.

Arrange on 8 skewers the chicken pieces, orange segments and the figs. Cook for 30 minutes, turning occasionally and basting with the chicken sauce.

39

Sosaties

SERVES 4

1 × 1 kg / 2 lb boned shoulder of lamb
40 g / 1½ oz butter
1 large onion, finely chopped
15 ml / 1 tbs curry powder or paste
10 ml / 2 tsp soft brown sugar
5 ml / 1 tsp salt
2.5 ml / ½ tsp black pepper
15 ml / 1 tbs fruit chutney
350 ml / 12 fl oz white wine vinegar
175 ml / 6 fl oz water
Finely grated rind of ½ lemon or
4 lemon leaves, coarsely chopped

With a sharp knife, trim the lamb of all fat. Cut the meat and the fat into small cubes. Thread the meat and fat alternately on to small metal skewers. Put the skewers in a shallow dish and set aside.

In a medium-sized frying pan, melt the butter over moderate heat. When the foam subsides, add the onion and fry, stirring occasionally, for 8–10 minutes or until it is golden brown. Add the curry powder or paste, sugar, salt, pepper and chutney and cook, stirring constantly, for 2 minutes. Pour in the vinegar and water and add the lemon rind or leaves. Bring to the boil, stirring occasionally.

Remove the pan from the heat and pour the mixture over the meat and fat cubes. Set aside to cool. When the marinade has cooled, cover the dish and place it in the refrigerator for 24 hours, turning the skewers occasionally.

Remove the skewers from the marinade and drain well. Reserve the marinade. Place the skewers on the barbecue and cook for 6–8 minutes, turning the skewers once, or until the meat is cooked.

Meanwhile, pour the marinade into a small saucepan. Place the pan over the fire and bring the marinade to the boil. Stirring occasionally, keep the sauce boiling for 8–10 minutes or until it has reduced by about one-third. Remove the pan from the heat and strain the sauce into a sauceboat (or directly onto individual servings).

Sosaties (above) and Neptune kebabs (right) are both marinated beforehand.

40

Remove the skewers from the heat. Arrange them on a heated platter and serve, with the sauce.

Sosaties are a traditional South African barbecue, or braaivleis, dish. The recipe was brought to South Africa by the Dutch settlers, who in turn adapted it from the Indonesian dish, Sate.

Kidney and chicken liver brochettes
SERVES 4–6
25g / 1 oz butter
700 / 1½ lb chicken livers
450 g / 1 lb lamb kidneys, trimmed of fat, skin and gristle and cut in half
450 g / 1 lb cooked ham, cut into 2.5 cm / 1 in cubes
6 medium-sized onions, peeled and quartered
2 green peppers, white pith and seeds removed and cut into 2.5 cm / 1 in squares
125 g / 4 oz melted butter

Melt the butter in a small frying pan. Add the chicken livers and fry them over moderate heat for 2–3 minutes. With a slotted spoon, remove the chicken livers from the pan. Drain them on kitchen paper towels and allow to cool.

Thread the chicken livers, kidneys, ham cubes, onion quarters and green pepper squares on metal skewers.

Using a pastry brush, coat the brochettes with half the melted butter. Place the brochettes on the barbecue and cook them for 4 minutes on each side, brushing them with melted butter again when you turn them.

Serve immediately.

Hot dog kebabs
SERVES 4
8 medium-sezed frankfurters, each cut into 4 pieces
800 g / 28 oz canned pineapple chunks, drained
8 bacon slices, rolled
8 small onions, peeled
2 green peppers, white pith removed, seeded and cut into pieces
50 g / 2 oz butter, melted

Thread the frankfurter pieces on to eight metal skewers, alternating with pineapple chunks, bacon rolls, onions and pieces of green pepper.

With a pastry brush, coat the kebabs with one-quarter of the melted butter and place them on the barbecue. Cook

for 15 minutes, turning frequently and basting with the remaining melted butter when they are turned.

Slide the kebabs off the skewers on to a heated serving dish and serve immediately, allowing 2 per person.

Neptune kebabs
SERVES 4
16 Dublin Bay prawns, shelled
2 small green peppers, white pith removed, seeded and cut into 16 equal-sized pieces
16 meium-sized mushrooms, wiped clean and stalks removed
16 sage leaves, washed and shaken dry
2 lemons, each cut into 8 sections
Marinade:
50 ml / 2 fl oz olive oil
30 ml / 2 tbs lemon juice
3 garlic cloves, crushed
5 ml / 1 tsp salt
2.5 ml / ½ tsp black pepper

In a large, shallow mixing bowl, combine all the marinade ingredients thoroughly. Add the shelled prawns, stirring well to coat them with the marinade. Set aside in a cool place to marinate for 1 hour, turning prawns over occasionally, during marinating time.

Remove the prawns from the marinade and pat them dry with kitchen paper towels. Reserve the marinade.

Thread each metal skewer with an alternating sequence of prawn, green pepper, a mushroom, one sage leaf and lemon wedge, until there are four of each on a skewer, allowing one skewer per person.

Place the skewers on the barbecue, basting them with a little of the reserved marinade. Cook them for 10 minutes, turning and basting occasionally.

Remove the kebabs from the barbecue. Slide them off the skewers and serve immediately on a warmed dish.

Mackerel kebabs
SERVES 4
4 mackerel, cleaned, gutted and backbones removed
6 button onions
4 small tomatoes
4 button mushrooms, wiped clean
1 large green pepper, white pith removed, seeded and cut into narrow strips
Marinade:
50 ml / 2 fl oz olive oil
2.5 ml / ½ tsp salt

1.25 ml / ¼ tsp black pepper
5 ml / 1 tsp dried oregano

Cut each mackerel into 4 or 5 slices.

Thread the slices of fish on to metal skewers, alternating with the onions, tomatoes, mushrooms and green pepper strips.

In a large shallow dish, combine the vinegar, olive oil, salt, pepper and oregano. Lay the prepared skewers in the dish and leave to marinate at room temperature for about 2 hours, turning occasionally.

When the fire is ready, remove the kebabs from the marinade and place them on the barbecue. Cook for 12–15 minutes, basting the kebabs with the marinade and turning them frequently, or until the fish flakes easily when tested with a fork.

Serve the kebabs immediately.

Scallop kebabs
SERVES 4
16 scallops, halved
8 slices lean bacon, rinds removed and halved lengthwise then across
16 button mushrooms, wiped clean and halved
16 button onions, halved
2 lemons, quartered
Marinade:
3 garlic cloves, crushed
60 ml / 4 tbs olive oil
30 ml / 1 tbs lemon juice
30 ml / 2 tbs dry sherry
5 ml / 1 tsp dried marjoram
5 ml / 1 tsp salt
2.5 ml / ½ tsp black pepper

First prepare the marinade. In a small mixing bowl, combine the garlic, olive oil, lemon juice, sherry, marjoram, salt and pepper, beating with a fork until they are thoroughly combined. Set aside.

Wrap each scallop half in a piece of bacon. Thread the scallop halves on to 8 skewers, alternating each one with a mushroom half and an onion. Lay the skewers in a large shallow dish, in one layer. Pour the marinade over the kebabs. Set aside for 30 minutes, turning the kebabs occasionally.

Remove the skewers from the marinade and place them on the barbecue. Reserve the marinade. Cook the kebabs for 10–12 minutes, turning frequently and basting with the reserved marinade, or until the bacon is crisp.

Remove the kebabs from the barbecue. Transfer them to a warmed serving dish, garnish with the lemon quarters and serve immediately.

The perfect accompaniment

No barbecue is complete without fresh, crisp salad and hot buttered bread, and this chapter contains a huge, mouth-watering selection of both. Salads can be prepared in advance and the bread, fresh of course, heated up just before serving. If you choose to be your own baker, there are recipes for hamburger rolls and pita, which is delicious filled with the 'fruits' of a barbecued kebab. Most of the salads have their own recipes for dressings, but there is also a special dressing section.

Below: Garlic bread and garlic salad.

Toss for a salad

Summer salad
SERVES 4

6 large lettuce leaves, washed and shaken dry
8 hard-boiled eggs, sliced
4 medium-sized tomatoes, washed and sliced
1 small green pepper, white pith removed, seeded and finely chopped
8 anchovy fillets
Dressing:
15 ml / 1 tbs finely chopped fresh parsley
1.25 ml / ¼ tsp dry mustard
1.25 ml / ¼ tsp salt
1.25 ml / ¼ tsp freshly ground black pepper
3 garlic cloves, crushed
60 ml / 4 tbs olive oil
15 ml / 1 tbs tarragon vinegar
15 ml / 1 tbs lemon juice

Arrange the lettuce leaves on a large serving plate.

Place the egg and tomato slices on the lettuce leaves, in alternating layers, beginning from the centre of the dish. Sprinkle on the chopped green pepper.

Roll up the anchovy fillets and arrange them on the outer edge of the dish.

To make the dressing, combine the parsley, mustard, salt, pepper and garlic cloves in a medium-sized mixing bowl. Slowly beat in the oil, vinegar and lemon juice. Combine the mixture thoroughly and pour it over the salad. With two large spoons, toss the salad.

Place the salad in the refrigerator to chill for 15 minutes before serving.

Fennel, chicory and tomato salad
SERVES 4–6

1 head of fennel, washed, trimmed and thinly sliced
1 head of chicory washed, outer leaves removed and thinly sliced
4 tomatoes, thinly sliced
Dressing:
60 ml / 4 tbs olive oil
30 ml / 2 tbs white wine vinegar
1 garlic clove, crushed
2.5 ml / ½ tsp salt

44

1.25 ml / ¼ tsp black pepper

Thinly slice the fennel and chicory and place them in a medium-sized serving dish. Add the tomatoes.

In a screw-top jar, combine the oil, vinegar, garlic, salt and pepper. Shake well and pour the dressing over the vegetables. Toss well and place the dish in the refrigerator.

Chill for at least 30 minutes before serving.

Radish, celery and cucumber salad
SERVES 3–4

225 g / 8 oz small radishes, trimmed
4 celery stalks, trimmed and cut into 6 mm / ¼ in lengths
½ small cucumber, diced
75 g / 3 oz cashew nuts
1.25 ml / ¼ tsp dried chervil
1.25 ml / ¼ tsp dried tarragon
Dressing:
1.25 ml / ¼ tsp salt
2.5 ml / ½ tsp black pepper
125 ml / 4 fl oz sour cream
15 ml / 1 tbs mayonnaise
15 ml / 1 tbs cider vinegar

In a medium-sized serving bowl, combine the radishes, celery, cucumber, cashew nuts, chervil and tarragon. Set aside.

In a small mixing bowl, combine the salt, pepper, sour cream, mayonnaise and vinegar, beating well with a fork until they are well blended. Pour the dressing over the vegetables and toss well until they are thoroughly coated.

Serve immediately or chill until it is required.

Fennel and cucumber salad
SERVES 4

1 cucumber, peeled and thinly sliced
1 head of fennel, cut into thin strips
4 radishes, thinly sliced
3 spring onions, finely chopped
Dressing:
45 ml / 3 tbs olive oil
15 ml / 1 tbs lemon juice
1 garlic clove, crushed
5 ml / 1 tsp salt
2.5 ml / ½ tsp black pepper
10 ml / 2 tsp chopped parsley

Place the cucumber, fennel, radishes and spring onions in a medium-sized serving dish.

In a small bowl, beat the olive oil, lemon juice, garlic, salt and pepper

together with a fork.

Pour the dressing over the mixture in the dish. Place the dish in the refrigerator and chill for at least 30 minutes. Just before serving, sprinkle over the parsley.

This delicious light summer salad goes particularly well with fish.

Spinach salad
SERVES 4

225 g / 8 oz spinach, coarsely chopped
8 lean bacon slices, rinds removed, grilled until crisp and coarsely chopped
2 large avocados, peeled, halved, stoned and chopped
Dressing:
90 ml / 6 tbs olive oil
5 ml / 1 tsp salt
5 ml / 1 tsp black pepper
2.5 ml / ½ tsp dry mustard
1 garlic clove, crushed
30 ml / 2 tbs white wine vinegar
15 ml / 1 tbs lemon juice

Place all of the salad ingredients in a large serving bowl and toss them together with two large spoons. Set aside.

Place all the dressing ingredients in a small mixing bowl and beat them together with a fork or a small wooden spoon until they are thoroughly blended.

Alternatively, place all the ingredients in a screw-top jar, screw on the lid and shake vigorously for 1 minute, or until the dressing is well blended.

Pour the dressing over the salad ingredients and toss well with the spoons until they are coated with the dressing. Serve immediately.

Watercress, fennel, cucumber and tomato salad
SERVES 4

1 bunch watercress, washed and shaken dry
½ fennel, trimmed and sliced
½ small cucumber, thinly sliced
4 tomatoes, quartered
6 anchovy fillets, halved
1 spring onion, trimmed and finely chopped
30 ml / 2 tbs chopped pimiento
75 ml / 3 fl oz French dressing (see recipe, this chapter)

In a large, deep serving platter or salad bowl, combine all the ingredients except the French dressing, tossing with two spoons until they are well mixed.

Pour the French dressing into the

mixture and, using the spoons, gently toss until all the ingredients are well coated. Serve at once.

Greek salad
SERVES 4–6
1 cos lettuce, outer leaves removed, inner leaves washed and separated
1 bunch of radishes, cleaned and sliced
225 g / 8 oz feta cheese, cut into cubes
1.25 ml / ¼ tsp dried marjoram
4 tomatoes, blanched, peeled and sliced
6 anchovies, drained and finely chopped
6 large black olives, halved and stoned
15 ml / 1 tbs chopped fresh parsley
2.5 ml / ½ tsp black pepper
Dressing:
60 ml / 4 tbs olive oil

22.5 ml / 4½ tsp white wine vinegar
15 ml / 1 tbs chopped mixed fresh herbs, such as marjoram, chives or lemon thyme
4 spring onions, chopped
5 ml / 1 tsp sugar
1.25 ml / ¼ tsp salt
2.5 ml / ½ tsp black pepper

Tear the lettuce leaves into pieces and arrange them on a large dish. Scatter the radish slices over the lettuce. Arrange the cheese in the centre of the dish and sprinkle it with the marjoram.

Place the tomatoes in a circle around the cheese and put the anchovies on top of the tomatoes, alternating with the olives. Sprinkle the parsley and pepper on top.

In a small bowl, mix together the oil, vinegar, fresh herbs, spring onions, sugar, salt and pepper.

Pour the dressing over the salad just before serving.

Coleslaw with caraway
SERVES 8
1 large white cabbage with coarse outer leaves removed, washed, cored and shredded
1 medium-sized onion, finely chopped
½ green pepper, white pith removed, seeded and finely chopped
2.5 ml / ½ tsp lemon juice
15 ml / 1 tbs caraway seeds
Dressing:
175 ml / 6 fl oz double cream
75 ml / 3 fl oz sour cream
15 ml / 1 tbs French mustard
45 ml / 3 tbs lemon juice
15 ml / 1 tbs sugar
2.5 ml / ½ tsp salt
1.25 ml / ¼ tsp white pepper

Below: Impress friends and family with this unusual and tasty salad of watercress, fennel, cucumber and tomato.

45

Arrange the shredded cabbage in a large serving dish and sprinkle with the onion, green pepper and lemon juice. Set aside.

In a medium-sized mixing bowl, mix together the double cream, sour cream, mustard and lemon juice, beating vigorously with a wooden spoon until the ingredients are thoroughly blended. Add the sugar, salt and pepper and mix well.

Pour the dressing over the shredded cabbage and add the caraway seeds to the mixture. Using 2 large spoons or forks, toss the cabbage mixture until it is completely saturated with dressing. Chill in the refrigerator for at least 1 hour and serve cold.

Caraway seeds provide interesting variation to this crisp coleslaw salad. It is a perfect accompaniment to barbecued chicken.

French bean salad

SERVES 4

½ kg / 1 lb fresh French beans, cooked in boiling, salted water, then rinsed in cold, running water
Dressing:
30 ml / 2 tbs wine vinegar
90 ml / 6 tbs olive oil
1.25 ml / ¼ tsp salt
Pinch of black pepper
2.5 ml / ½ tsp prepared mustard
5 ml / 1 tsp finely chopped fresh dill
5 ml / 1 tsp finely chopped fresh parsley
1 garlic clove, crushed

Make the dressing by combining all the ingredients in a screw-top jar. Shake vigorously until they are well mixed.

Place the beans in a large mixing bowl. Pour the dressing over the beans and mix well to coat them thoroughly.

Cool, then place the bowl of dressed beans in the refrigerator and chill the salad well before serving.

It is important for the French beans not to be overcooked — that is, they should be crisp but never limp. The cooking time depends on the quality and type of French beans used and will take from 5 to 15 minutes.

Mushroom and mint salad

SERVES 4–6

½ kg / 1 lb new potatoes, cooked, diced and cooled
125 g / 4 oz frozen peas, cooked, drained and cooled
175 g / 6 oz button mushrooms, wiped clean and sliced

46

Dressing:
225 ml / 8 fl oz yogurt
30 ml / 2 tbs finely chopped fresh mint
2.5 ml / ½ tsp salt
1.25 ml / ¼ tsp white pepper

Place the potatoes, peas and mushrooms in a large salad bowl.

In a medium-sized mixing bowl, mix the yogurt, mint, salt and pepper together with a wooden spoon. Pour the dressing over the vegetables. Using two large spoons, toss the salad until the vegetables are thoroughly coated with the dressing.

Place the bowl in the refrigerator and chill for 1 hour before serving.

Hot potato salad

SERVES 8

1 kg / 2 lb potatoes, cooked, cut into cubes or strips and kept warm
1 large dill pickle, finely chopped
1 small onion, finely chopped
5 ml / 1 tsp dried dill
15 ml / 1 tbs chopped fresh parsley
300 ml / 10 fl oz mayonnaise

Put the potatoes into a large salad bowl. Add the pickle, onion, dill and parsley and mix well to blend.

Pour over the mayonnaise while potatoes are still warm and, using two large spoons, toss carefully to coat the potatoes.

Serve at once, or keep warm in a low oven before serving.

Tabboulch
(Wheat and tomato salad)

SERVES 6

225 g / 8 oz cracked wheat, soaked in cold water for 20 minutes and drained
60 ml / 4 tbs chopped fresh parsley
30 ml / 2 tbs chopped fresh mint
1 medium-sized onion, finely chopped
3 spring onions, trimmed and finely chopped
½ kg / 1 lb tomatoes, coarsely chopped
5 ml / 1 tsp salt
10 ml / 2 tsp black pepper
50 ml / 2 fl oz lemon juice
75 ml / 3 fl oz olive oil
10 lettuce leaves, washed and shaken dry
4 tomatoes, quartered

In a medium-sized mixing bowl, mix together the wheat, three-quarters of the parsley, the mint, onion, spring onions

and chopped tomatoes until they are thoroughly combined. Set aside.

In a small mixing bowl, combine the salt, pepper, lemon juice and oil, beating well with a kitchen fork. Pour the dressing over the salad and toss well, using two large spoons.

Line a medium-sized salad bowl with the lettuce leaves and arrange the salad in the middle. Garnish with the tomato quarters and remaining parsley before serving.

Tabboulch (tah-boolsh) is an adaptation of a traditional Arabian dish. It may be served as an hors d'oeuvre or as an accompaniment to spiced meat or chicken. Cracked wheat is available from most health food stores.

French potato salad

SERVES 4

½ kg / 1 lb potatoes, cooked, peeled and thinly sliced
2 small onions, thinly sliced and pushed out into rings
5 ml / 1 tsp salt
3.75 ml / ¾ tsp black pepper
15 ml / 1 tbs chopped chives
Dressing:
45 ml / 3 tbs olive oil
30 ml / 2 tbs white wine vinegar

Arrange the potato slices and onion rings in alternating layers in a serving dish. Sprinkle each layer with a little of the salt, pepper and chives.

In a screw-top jar, combine the olive oil and vinegar and shake well. Pour the dressing over the potatoes and onions. Cover the dish and place it in the refrigerator. Chill for 8 hours before serving.

Mushroom salad

SERVES 4

225 g / 8 oz button mushrooms, wiped clean and thinly sliced
50 g / 2 oz cooked peas
1 crisp head of lettuce, outer leaves removed, washed and shredded
Dressing:
45 ml / 3 tbs olive oil
15 ml / 1 tbs fresh lemon juice
1.25 ml / ¼ tsp salt
Pinch of black pepper

In a screwtop jar, combine the oil, lemon juice, salt and pepper. Shake the dressing well.

Right: Two salads for a summer barbecue.

Place the mushroom and peas in a mixing bowl and pour over the dressing. Toss well and place the dish in the refrigerator. Chill for 30 minutes.

Line a medium-sized serving dish with the lettuce. Remove the mushroom and pea mixture from the refrigerator and pile it into the centre of the leaves. Serve at once.

Potato salad
SERVES 4
½ kg / 1 lb potatoes, cooked, peeled and sliced
30 ml / 2 tbs chopped fresh chives
60 ml / 4 tbs chopped leek greens
Dressing:
125 ml / 4 fl oz mayonnaise
15 ml / 1 tbs lemon juice
15 ml / 1 tbs olive oil
5 ml / 1 tsp salt
2.5 ml / ½ tsp black pepper

Place three-quarters of the potatoes in a medium-sized mixing bowl. Pour over the mayonnaise and sprinkle with the lemon juice, oil, salt, pepper and half of the chives. Using two large spoons, carefully toss the potatoes until they are thoroughly coated with the mayonnaise mixture.

Spoon the mixture into a serving bowl. Arrange the remaining potato slices over the top of the salad. Sprinkle with the remaining chives and scatter the leeks around the edge of the bowl.

Cover the bowl and place it in the refrigerator to chill for at least 30 minutes before serving.

Rice salad with garlic sausage
SERVES 4–6
125 g / 4 oz long-grain rice, washed, soaked in cold water for
30 minutes and drained
7.5 ml / 1½ tsp salt
2.5 ml / ½ tsp black pepper
75 ml / 3 fl oz mayonnaise
5 ml / 1 tsp dried chervil
½ red pepper, white pith removed, seeded and chopped
2 hard-boiled eggs
1 small lettuce, outer leaves removed and inner leaves washed, separated and shaken dry
1 × 20 cm / 8 in garlic sausage, cut into 6 mm / ¼ in thick slices

Put the rice in a saucepan. Pour over enough water to cover the rice and add 5 ml / 1 tsp of the salt. Bring the water to the boil over high heat and cover the pan. Reduce the heat to very low and simmer for 15 minutes or until all the liquid has been absorbed and the rice is tender. Remove the pan from the heat. Transfer the rice to a large mixing bowl and set aside to cool for 5 minutes.

Meanwhile, in a small mixing bowl, combine the remaining salt, the pepper, mayonnaise and chervil.

Pour half the mayonnaise mixture over the rice and add the red pepper. Using two spoons, toss the rice mixture until it is well coated with the mayonnaise. Set aside to cool completely.

Meanwhile, cut the hard-boiled eggs in half, remove the yolks and add them to the remaining mayonnaise mixture. Mash the yolks into the mayonnaise mixture and beat well. Spoon the mayonnaise mixture into the cavities of the egg whites left by the yolks.

Arrange the lettuce leaves in a salad bowl. Pile the rice mixture on top. Arrange the sausage slices and filled egg whites around the rice. Serve immediately.

Right: Chopped chives and leek greens give potato salad its distinctive flavour, while the rice salad (below) depends upon garlic sausage and olives.

Tangy dressings

French dressing
MAKES ABOUT 125 ML / 4 FL OZ
90 ml / 6 tbs olive oil
5 ml / 1 tsp salt
5 ml / 1 tsp black pepper
30 ml / 2 tbs wine vinegar

In a small mixing bowl, beat the oil, salt and pepper with a fork. Gradually beat in the vinegar. Use as required.

N.B. The classic French dressing consists of olive oil, wine vinegar, salt and pepper. As a variation crushed garlic, mustard and/or chopped herbs may also be added, in which case the dressing becomes sauce vinaigrette, or vinaigrette dressing.

Roquefort dressing
MAKES ABOUT 225 ML / 8 FL OZ
225 ml / 8 fl oz French dressing
50 g / 2 oz Roquefort cheese, finely crumbled
15 ml / 1 tbs chopped fresh chives

Place the French dressing in a medium-sized mixing bowl and mash in the cheese until the mixture is thoroughly combined. Stir in the chives.
Either use the dressing immediately or pour it into a screw-top jar and chill in the refrigerator until required.

Mint dressing
MAKES ABOUT 75 ML / 3 FL OZ
45 ml / 3 tbs olive oil
15 ml / 1 tbs lemon juice
2.5 ml / ½ tsp salt
2.5 ml / ½ tsp black pepper
15 ml / 1 tbs finely chopped fresh mint
10 ml / 2 tsp sugar

In a small mixing bowl, combine all the ingredients and mix well with a wooden spoon. Alternatively place all the ingredients in a screw-top jar and shake well.
Place the dressing in the refrigerator to chill for 30 minutes before serving.

A cool, refreshing dressing, this is perfect on a tomato or potato salad.

Right: Mayonnaise.

Thousand Island dressing
MAKES 600 ML / 1 PINT
425 ml / 16 fl oz mayonnaise
6.25 ml / 1¼ tsp Tabasco sauce
30 ml / 2 tbs chopped pimientos or sweet pickle
10 stuffed green olives, finely chopped
2 hard-boiled eggs, finely chopped
1 shallot, very finely chopped
50 ml / 2 fl oz French dressing

In a large bowl beat all the ingredients together with a wooden spoon, until they are thoroughly combined.
Pour the dressing into a serving bowl and chill in the refrigerator for at least 1 hour before serving.

Mayonnaise
MAKES 300 ML / 10 FL OZ
2 egg yolks, at room temperature
2.5 ml / ½ tsp salt
2.5 ml / ½ tsp dry mustard
Pinch of white pepper
300 ml / 10 fl oz olive oil, at room

temperature
15 ml / 1 tbs lemon juice or white wine vinegar

Place the egg yolks, salt, mustard and pepper in a medium-sized mixing bowl. Using a wire whisk beat the ingredients until they are thoroughly blended and have thickened. Add the oil, a few drops at a time, whisking constantly. Do not add the oil too quickly or the mayonnaise will curdle.

Once the mayonnaise has thickened the oil may be added a little more rapidly.

Beat in a few drops of lemon juice or vinegar from time to time to prevent the mayonnaise from becoming too thick. When all the oil has been added, stir in the remaining vinegar or lemon juice.

Taste the sauce for seasoning and add more salt, mustard and vinegar if desired.

To make a garlic mayonnaise, or aioli sauce, add 4 cloves of crushed garlic to the 15 ml / 1 tbs of lemon juice or vinegar and mix thoroughly, adding to the egg mixture as described above for the lemon juice.

If the oil is added to the egg yolks too quickly initially, and the mixture curdles, reconstitute the mixture by placing another egg yolk and the given seasonings in another bowl and beating well. Gradually add the curdled mixture to the fresh egg yolk, beating constantly, until the mixture thickens; then add the mixture a little more quickly until it is all absorbed.

When making mayonnaise it is important to use fresh eggs as they have a greater ability to hold the oil in a stable emulsion.

For a lighter, less rich mayonnaise, use whole eggs instead of just egg yolks.

Coleslaw dressing with yogurt
MAKES 350 ML / 12 FL OZ
300 ml / 10 fl oz mayonnaise
60 ml / 4 tbs yogurt
5 ml / 1 tsp sugar
2.5 ml / ½ tsp salt
15 ml / 1 tbs grated onion
15 ml / 1 tbs finely chopped celery

Blend the mayonnaise with the yogurt, mixing well with a wooden spoon. Add the remaining dressing ingredients and beat for 1 minute. Use immediately.

Bread for perfection

Herb bread
SERVES 6
1 large French loaf
175 g / 6 oz butter
1 garlic clove, crushed
15 ml / 1 tbs finely chopped fresh parsley
1.25 ml / ¼ tsp dried sage
15 ml / 1 tbs very finely chopped fresh chives

Preheat the oven to 190°C, 375°F, Gas Mark 5.

Using a sharp knife, slice the bread downwards at 2.5 cm / 1 in intervals to within 6 mm / ¼ in of the base, so that each slice is still attached to the bottom of the crust. Set aside.

In a small mixing bowl, cream the butter with a wooden spoon until it is smooth and creamy. Beat in the garlic, parsley, sage, chives and black pepper. Continue beating until the mixture is smooth and evenly coloured.

With a knife, spread equal amounts of the herb butter on to the bread slices, being careful not to detach them.

Wrap the loaf in aluminium foil and place it on a large baking sheet. Place the loaf in the centre of the oven and bake for 15–20 minutes, or until the loaf is very hot and the butter has melted into the bread.

Remove the loaf from the oven. Remove and discard the foil. Break the loaf into slices and serve immediately.

Garlic bread
SERVES 6–8
225 g / 8 oz butter, softened
30 ml / 2 tbs finely chopped fresh parsley
2 garlic cloves, very finely chopped
2 long loaves of French bread

Preheat the oven to fairly hot 200°C, 400°F, Gas Mark 6.

In a small mixing bowl, cream the butter, parsley and garlic together with a wooden spoon. With a large knife, thickly slice the loaves crosswise to within about 6 mm / ¼ in of the bottom.

Spread the butter mixture generously on one side of each of the slices. Wrap the loaves in aluminium foil and place them on a baking sheet in the centre of the oven. Bake for 15–20 minutes, or until the bread is very crusty and the butter has melted.

Remove the loaves from the oven and serve immediately, in the foil.

An excellent accompaniment for any barbecue, garlic bread is very simple to make.

Herb bread crisps
SERVES 4–6
75 g / 3 oz butter
5 ml / 1 tsp lemon juice
2.5 ml / ½ tsp dried chervil
2.5 ml / ½ tsp dried tarragon
2.5 ml / ½ tsp chopped fresh parsley
1.25 ml / ¼ tsp dried thyme
2.5 ml / ½ tsp chopped fresh chives
1 small garlic clove, crushed
6 slices of bread or 12 slices of French bread

Preheat the oven to 180°C, 350°F, Gas Mark 4.

In a medium-sized mixing bowl, cream the butter with a wooden spoon until it is fairly soft. Beat the lemon juice into the butter, then the chervil, tarragon, parsley, thyme, chives and garlic.

Spread the butter mixture on the bread slices. If the slices are large, cut them in half diagonally. Place them on a baking sheet. Place the baking sheet in the oven and bake the bread for 20 minutes or until it is golden brown and crisp.

Remove the baking sheet from the oven and place the bread in a folded napkin in a basket. Serve immediately.

N.B. A fresh white loaf or rolls can be substituted for French bread. Whatever bread you choose, these herb-flavoured snacks are ideal for serving in or with soup or with salads and crudité.

Hamburger rolls
MAKES 8 ROLLS
450 g / 1 lb flour
2.5 ml / ½ tsp salt
150 ml / 5 fl oz plus 30 ml / 2 tbs milk
150 ml / 5 fl oz water
5 ml / 1 tsp sugar
15 ml / 1 tbs dried yeast
50 g / 2 oz butter

Sift the flour and salt into a large mixing bowl. Put in a warm place.

Warm the water and all but 30 ml / 2 tbs of the milk, place in a bowl and add the sugar. Sprinkle the yeast on top. Leave in a warm place for 5 minutes or until it is frothy.

Rub the butter into the warm flour-and-salt mixture. Make a well in the middle of the flour and pour in the frothy yeast mixture. With your hands, mix into a soft dough, adding 5–10 ml / 1–2 tsp more warm water if necessary.

Place the dough in a greased bowl, cover with a clean cloth and leave it to stand in a warm place for 1 hour or more until it doubles in size.

Preheat the oven to 220°C, 425°F, Gas Mark 7.

Grease a baking tin with a little butter and dust with flour. Remove the risen dough from the bowl and knead it on a floured surface. Divide it into 8 equal pieces. Knead each piece separately and pat each into an oval shape. Flatten each piece, place on the baking tin and leave in a warm place for 15 minutes.

Brush each roll with the remaining milk and bake in the oven for 15–20 minutes. Serve hot.

Pita (Greek or Arabian bread)
MAKES 12

15 g / ½ oz fresh yeast
30 ml / 2 tbs plus 5 ml / 1 tsp sugar
600 ml / 1 pint plus 15 ml /
1 tbs lukewarm water
675 g / 1½ lb strong white flour
15 ml / 1 tbs salt
5 ml / 1 tsp olive oil

Crumble the yeast into a small bowl and mash in 5 ml / 1 tsp of sugar with a kitchen fork. Add 15 ml / 1 tbs of water and cream the water and yeast together to form a smooth paste. Set the bowl aside in a warm, draught-free place for 15–20 minutes, or until the yeast has risen and is puffed up and frothy.

Sift the flour, the remaining sugar and the salt into a warmed, large mixing bowl. Make a well in the centre of the flour mixture and pour in the yeast and the remaining lukewarm water. Using your hands or a spatula, gradually draw the flour into the liquid. Continue mixing until all the flour is incorporated and the dough comes away from the sides of the bowl.

Turn the dough out on to a floured board or marble slab and knead for about 10 minutes, re-flouring the surface if the dough becomes sticky. The dough should be elastic and smooth.

Rinse, thoroughly dry and lightly grease the large mixing bowl. Shape the dough into a ball and return it to the bowl. With a pastry brush, lightly coat the top of the dough with the oil. Cover the bowl with a clean, damp cloth. Set the bowl in a warm, draught-free place and leave it for 1½ hours, or until the dough has risen and almost doubled in bulk.

Turn the dough out of the bowl on to a floured surface and knead it for 4 minutes. Using a sharp knife, cut the dough into 12 equal pieces and shape each piece into a ball. Place the balls on a large baking sheet, cover with a damp cloth and return to a warm place for 10 minutes.

Place three baking sheets in the oven. Preheat the oven to 230°C, 450°F, Gas Mark 8.

On a floured surface, roll the balls of dough out into circles, approximately 12.5 cm / 5 in in diameter.

Remove the hot baking sheets from the oven. Place 2 circles of dough on each sheet. Return the baking sheets to the oven. Bake the dough circles for 8–10 minutes or until the bread is puffed up and golden brown.

Remove the baking sheets from the oven. Transfer the bread to a towel spread over your working surface to cool and flatten. Bake the remaining dough in the same way.

Serve the pitas slightly warm.

N.B. The secret of making pita is to heat the baking trays at the same time as the oven is being heated, so that the dough is baked on a very hot tray. This causes the bread to puff up immediately and creates a hollow flat bread. Pita may be stored in a plastic bag in the refrigerator for up to a week or for several months in a home freezer. Before eating pita, heat it in a hot oven or place it on foil over the barbecue.

Pita makes a wonderful envelope for kebabs and a very good 'scoop' for taramasalata.

Left: Hamburger rolls straight from your oven can not fail to delight the hungry barbecue hordes.

Right, from left: Herb bread crisps baked to a golden brown, and herb bread sandwiched with herbal butter and ready for foil and oven.

Just desserts

And for the final flourishing touch — assuming there is still room — here are some tantalizing desserts. Everything from summer strawberry shortcake to delectable fruit kebabs, but be careful not to burn your tongue! You might find that you need a short breather between the main course and sweet, in which case this would be an excellent time to do some preliminary clearing away. By the time the dishes have been stacked in the kitchen and the left-over food has been stored, you should find your appetite is back and ready for more goodies. The desserts are divided into three sections to help you choose the one that will complement your main course most. Enjoy your selection.

From top: Lemon manqué and lemon meringue pie.

Pretty fancy

Pavlova
SERVES 8
**5 egg whites
275 g / 10 oz plus 15 ml / 1 tbs caster
sugar
10 ml / 2 tsp cornflour, sifted
2.5 ml / ½ tsp vanilla essence
5 ml / 1 tsp malt vinegar
5 ml / 1 tsp orange-flavoured
liqueur
300 ml / 10 fl oz double cream,
stiffly whipped
450 g / 1 lb fresh or canned and
drained fruit**

Preheat the oven to 150°C, 300°F, Gas
Mark 2. With a pencil draw a 22.5 cm
/ 9 in circle (use a plate as a guide) on a
piece of non-stick silicone paper and
place this on a baking sheet. Set aside.

In a large mixing bowl, beat the egg
whites with a wire whisk or rotary beater
until they form stiff peaks. Beat in 125 g /
4 oz of the caster sugar and continue
beating for 1 minute or until the mixture
is very stiff and glossy. Using a metal
spoon, fold in all but 15 ml / 1 tbs of the
remaining sugar, the cornflour, vanilla
essence and vinegar.

Spoon one-third of the mixture on to
the circle of paper to make a base about
6 mm / ¼ in thick. Fill a forcing bag,
fitted with a 2.5 cm / 1 in nozzle, with the
remaining mixture and pipe it around the
edge of the circle in decorative swirls, to
form a case to hold the filling.

Place the baking sheet in the oven and
bake for 1 hour. Turn off the oven and
leave the meringue in the oven for a
further 30 minutes, or until it is crisp on
the outside but still soft in the centre.

Remove the baking sheet from the oven.
Leave the meringue to cool completely.
When it is cold, lift it off the baking sheet
and carefully remove and discard the
paper from the bottom.

Place the meringue case on a serving
plate. Fold the orange-flavoured liqueur
and the remaining 15 ml / 1 tbs of sugar
into the cream. Spoon the cream into the
centre of the meringue case and pile the
fruit on top of the cream. Serve at once.

N.B. Pavlova should be crisp on the outside, but soft and creamy in the centre.
Fresh, exotic fruits such as passion fruit,
pineapples and Chinese gooseberries go
beautifully with the soft meringue, but
any fresh or canned fruit may be used.

Lemon manqué
SERVES 8
**4 eggs, separated
Grated rind and juice of 2 lemons
50 g / 2 oz plus 5 ml / 1 tsp butter,
melted
75 g / 3 oz plus 30 ml / 2 tbs
flour
30 ml / 2 tbs rum
Meringue:
3 egg whites
175 g / 6 oz caster
sugar
Grated rind of 1 lemon
50 g / 2 oz pistachio nuts,
crushed**

Preheat the oven to 180°C, 350°F, Gas
Mark 4.

With the 5 ml / 1 tsp of melted butter,
lightly grease a 22.5 cm / 9 in moule à
manqué cake tin (a round tin similar to a
sandwich tin, with sloping sides,
3.7–5 cm / 1½–2 in deep). Sprinkle
the tin with the 30 ml / 2 tbs flour,
knocking out any excess. Set aside.

In a medium-sized mixing bowl, beat
the egg yolks and sugar with a wire whisk
or rotary beater until the mixture is thick
and pale yellow in colour. Add the lemon
rind and juice and continue beating until
well mixed.

In another mixing bowl, beat the egg
whites with a wire whisk or rotary beater
until they form stiff peaks.

Using the metal spoon, fold the egg
whites into the egg yolks and sugar
mixture, sifting in the remaining flour at
the same time. Quickly mix in the remaining butter and rum. Turn the mixture
into the cake tin. Place the tin in the oven
and bake for 30–35 minutes, or until the
cake has risen, is lightly browned and the
centre springs back when lightly pressed
with the fingertips.

Remove the cake from the oven and
allow it to cool in the tin for 6–8 minutes.
Run a knife around the edge of the tin
and reverse the cake on to a wire cake
rack, giving the tin a light tap on the
bottom. Turn the cake over immediately
so that the top is uppermost. Leave to
cool for about 30 minutes before covering
it with the meringue.

Preheat the oven to 230°C, 450°F, Gas
Mark 8.

While the cake is cooling, prepare the
meringue. In a large mixing bowl, beat
the egg whites with a wire whisk or rotary
beater until they are almost stiff. Add
15 ml / 1 tbs of the sugar and continue
beating for 1 minute or until the egg
whites form stiff peaks. With a metal
spoon, quickly fold in the remaining

sugar and the lemon rind.

Using a spatula, cover the outside of
the cake with the meringue mixture.
Sprinkle the pistachio nuts over the
meringue. Place the cake in the centre of
the oven and bake for 4–6 minutes, or
until the meringue turns a pale golden
colour. Serve cold.

55

Cakes, pies and flans

Strawberry shortcake
SERVES 4–8
225 g / 8 oz flour
50 g / 2 oz icing sugar
175 g / 6 oz butter,
softened
1 egg yolk
300 ml / 10 fl oz double
cream
30 ml / 2 tbs caster sugar

½ kg / 1 lb strawberries, hulled and washed

Lightly grease two baking sheets. Set aside.

Sift with flour and icing sugar into a medium-sized mixing bowl. With a table knife, cut the remaining butter into small pieces and add it to the mixture in the bowl.

Using your hands, mix the flour mixture and butter together until the mixture resembles fine breadcrumbs. With the knife, stir in the egg yolk and 30 ml / 2 tbs of the cream. Mix very well and form the dough into a ball. Cover the dough with greaseproof or waxed paper and place it in the refrigerator to chill for

30 minutes.

Preheat the oven to 190°C, 375°F, Gas Mark 5.

Divide the dough into two equal pieces. On a floured surface, roll out each piece into a 22.5 cm / 9 in circle.

Place the two circles on the prepared baking sheets and place them in the oven. Bake for 12–15 minutes or until the edges of the shortcakes are golden brown.

Remove the sheets from the oven and carefully transfer the shortcakes to a wire rack to cool.

Meanwhile, thinly slice the strawberries. In a medium-sized mixing bowl, beat the remaining cream and the sugar with a wire whisk or rotary beater until the mixture forms stiff peaks.

Redcurrant flan, filled with crème pâtissière.

Left: *Strawberry shortcake.*

Lightly fold the strawberries into the cream. Spoon the mixture into a heap in the centre of one of the shortcakes.

With a sharp knife, cut the other circle into eight equal triangles. Pile the triangles up against the strawberry mixture and serve at once.

Redcurrant flan
SERVES 8
400 ml / 15 fl oz creme pâtissiere (see following recipe)
15 ml / 1 tbs cherry brandy
1 × 22.5 cm / 9 in flan case made with shortcrust pastry, baked blind and cooled (see final recipe this section)
550 g / 1¼ lb redcurrants, trimmed

30 ml / 2 tbs sugar
175 ml / 6 fl oz raspberry jelly, cool and on the point of setting
300 ml / 10 fl oz double cream, stiffly whipped

In a medium-sized mixing bowl, combine the crème pâtissière and cherry brandy.

Spoon the crème pâtissière mixture into the flan case. Arrange about 450 g / 1 lb of the redcurrants on top of the mixture and sprinkle over the sugar. Spoon the cooled raspberry jelly over the redcurrants. Place the flan in the refrigerator for 1 hour or until the jelly has set.

Remove the flan from the refrigerator. Spread the whipped cream over the top of the flan. Decorate with the remaining redcurrants and serve immediately.

Creme pâtissière
MAKES 550 ML / 1 PINT
2 large eggs, separated
100 g / 4 oz caster
sugar
50 g / 2 oz flour
15 ml / 1 tbs cornflour
550 ml / 1 pint milk
2.5 / ½ tsp vanilla essence

In a medium-sized bowl lightly beat the egg yolks with a fork. Add the sugar and beat the mixture until it is creamy. Sift in both the cornflour and the flour a little at a time, beating constantly, then gradually mix in the vanilla essence and 150 ml / 5 fl oz of the milk.

In a medium-sized saucepan, scald the remaining milk over high heat. Pour the hot milk into the egg-and-sugar mixture, beating well with a wire whisk. Return the mixture to the pan and, stirring constantly, bring it back to the boil. Remove the pan from the heat and beat the mixture until it is smooth. Set it aside and allow it to cool.

In a small bowl, whisk the egg white with a wire whisk until it is stiff. Transfer about one-quarter of the warm cream mixture to a medium-sized bowl. Carefully fold the egg white into the mixture. Fold the egg-white mixture into the remaining cream in the saucepan. Return the saucepan to the stove and cook the mixture over low heat for 2 minutes, stirring occasionally.

Pour the cream into a bowl to cool before using it.

N.B. Crème pâtissière is sometimes known as pastry or confectioners' custard.

Lemon meringue pie
SERVES 8
1 × 22.5 cm / 9 in flan case made from rich shortcrust pastry, baked blind and cooled (see final recipe, this section)
Filling:
Juice and finely grated rind of 2 lemons
300 ml / 10 fl oz water
50 g / 2 oz caster sugar
45 ml / 3 tbs arrowroot, dissolved in 30 ml / 2 tbs water
4 egg yolks, lightly beaten
Meringue:
4 egg whites
175 g / 6 oz caster sugar

Preheat the oven to moderate 180°C, 350°F, Gas Mark 4.

To make the filling, in a medium-sized saucepan, combine the lemon juice, rind, water and sugar.

Set the pan over moderate heat and cook the mixture, stirring frequently, until the sugar has dissolved. Stir in the dissolved arrowroot and continue cooking, stirring frequently for 5 minutes, or until the mixture is thick.

Remove the pan from the heat and allow the mixture to cool to lukewarm, then beat in the egg yolks.

Spoon the lemon and egg yolk mixture into the pastry case, smoothing it down with a flat-bladed knife. Place the case in the oven and bake for 5 minutes or until the filling has set.

To make the meringue, in a medium-sized mixing bowl, using a wire whisk or rotary beater, beat the egg whites until
58

frothy. Gradually beat in the sugar and continue beating until the meringue mixture forms stiff peaks.

Pile the meringue on top of the lemon filling, to cover it completely. Place the pie in the centre of the oven and bake for 20–25 minutes, or until the meringue has set and is golden brown on top.

Remove the pie from the oven and serve immediately, or cool and serve.

N.B. The secret of a good lemon meringue pie is the contrast between the tangy lemon filling and the sweet meringue topping — so don't oversweeten the filling. The amount of sugar given in this recipe is just right for good-sized juicy lemons.

Pineapple cheesecake
SERVES 8–10
125 g / 4 oz butter
225 g / 8 oz crushed shortbread biscuits
30 ml / 2 tbs caster sugar
2.5 ml / ½ tsp ground allspice
Filling:
1¼ kg / 2½ lb ricotta cheese
50 g / 2 oz caster sugar
30 ml / 2 tbs flour
2.5 ml / ½ tsp vanilla essence
Very finely grated rind of 2 small lemons
Pinch ground allspice
3 egg yolks
1 large fresh pineapple, peeled, cored and very finely chopped
6 walnuts, sliced in half

Preheat the oven to 180°C, 350°F, Gas Mark 4.

Lightly grease a 22.5 cm / 9 in loose-bottomed cake tin. Set it aside.

In a medium-sized saucepan, melt the butter over moderate heat. Remove the pan from the heat and add the crushed biscuits, caster sugar and allspice. Beat the mixture with a wooden spoon until the biscuit crumbs are thoroughly coated with the melted butter.

Spoon the mixture into the prepared cake tin. Using the back of the spoon or your fingers, press the mixture down so that it evenly lines the bottom of the tin. Set aside.

To make the filling, place the ricotta cheese in a large fine wire strainer held over a medium-sized mixing bowl. Using the back of a wooden spoon, rub the cheese through the strainer. Add the sugar, flour, vanilla essence, lemon rind and allspice. Beat the mixture with the

wooden spoon until it is well blended. Beat in the egg yolks, one at a time, beating until the mixture is smooth.

Spoon half of the filling over the biscuit mixture base. Using a flat-bladed knife or the back of the spoon, spread the filling evenly over the base. Spoon over the chopped pineapple and spread it over the filling. Spoon over the remaining ricotta filling and smooth it over the pineapple to cover it completely.

Place the tin in the centre of the oven and bake the cheesecake for 20 minutes.

Remove the cheesecake from the oven and arrange the walnuts decoratively over the top.

Return the cheesecake to the oven and bake for a further 10–15 minutes or until the filling is firm.

Remove the cheesecake from the oven and set it aside to cool completely. Then lift off the sides of the tin. Very carefully slide the cheesecake off the base of the tin on to a chilled serving plate.

Place the cheesecake in the refrigerator and chill for at least 1 hour before serving.

Shortcrust pastry
MAKES 225 G / 8 OZ
225 g / 8 oz flour
2.5 ml / ½ tsp salt
50 g / 2 oz butter or margarine
50 g / 2 oz vegetable fat
45–60 ml / 3–4 tbs iced water

Sift the flour and salt into a medium-sized mixing bowl. Add the butter and vegetable fat to the bowl and cut them into small pieces with a table knife. With your fingertips, rub the fat into the flour until the mixture resembles coarse breadcrumbs.

Add 45 ml / 3 tbs of the iced water and, using the knife, mix it into the flour mixture. With your hands, mix and knead the dough until it is smooth. Add more water if the dough is too dry. Form the dough into a ball, wrap it in greaseproof or waxed paper and chill it in the refrigerator for 30 minutes to let it 'rest'.

The dough is now ready to use. When rolling it out, place it on a lightly floured, cool if possible, working surface and use a floured rolling pin. Make sure that the dough does not stick to the surface as it is rolled out.

Roll the dough lightly away from you, until it is of an even thickness, about 6 mm / ¼ in, but do not stretch it to shape.

Line the flan ring or pie dish and trim off any excess dough.

N.B. To bake blind, bake the pastry shells without their fillings.

After lining the pie dish or flan ring with the rolled-out pastry, prick the base of the shell all over with a fork. Then line it with crumpled foil or greaseproof paper, filled with dried beans or uncooked rice, kept specially for this purpose. (They act as a weight.)

Preheat the oven to 200°C, 400°F, Gas Mark 6.

Bake the prepared pie shell for 10 minutes in the centre of the oven. At the end of this period, take the shell out of the oven.

Reduce temperature to 180°C, 350°F, Gas Mark 4.

Remove the foil, or paper, and beans.

Continue baking for a further 10 minutes, so that the pastry can colour slightly.

Allow the pastry to cool completely before adding ingredients for the pie or flan filling.

Below: Pineapple cheesecake might take some time to prepare, but the end product is worth every minute.

Fruit kebabs

Roasted apples on skewers

SERVES 8

8 dessert apples
The sauce:
50 g / 2 oz butter
60 ml / 4 tbs gin (optional)
90 ml / 6 tbs grapefruit juice
45 ml / 3 tbs sugar

Secure the apples on 8 metal skewers and cook over the fire, for 15–30 minutes depending upon their size, turning frequently.

Make the sauce by melting the butter in a small pan and stirring in the other ingredients until the sugar is dissolved. Keep the sauce warm and accessible for people to dip their apples into before eating.

Kebabs with fruit

SERVES 6

12 canned apricot halves, drained
6 large bananas, cut into thirds
2 pears, peeled and thickly sliced
2 oranges, peeled and separated into segments
12 canned pineapple chunks, drained
25 g / 1 oz butter, melted
15 ml / 1 tbs brown sugar
Marinade:
125 ml / 4 fl oz orange juice
125 ml / 4 fl oz lemon juice
30 ml / 2 tbs orange-flavoured liqueur
5 ml / 1 tsp finely chopped fresh mint
30 ml / 2 tbs clear honey

In a large dish, combine the orange juice, lemon juice, orange-flavoured liqueur, mint and honey. Add the fruit and allow the mixture to marinate for at least 1 hour.

With a slotted spoon, lift the fruit out of the marinade and thread it on to eight metal skewers. Reserve the marinade.

With a pastry brush, coat the kebabs with the melted butter and sprinkle them with the brown sugar. Place them on the barbecue and grill for 6–8 minutes, turning them frequently so that the fruit does not burn.

In a small saucepan heat the reserved marinade over the fire. As soon as the mixture is hot, but not boiling, pour it into a sauceboat and keep warm to serve with the kebabs.

N.B. At this stage, it really is fun if your guests each cook their own kebab.

A cool clean taste

Pineapple delight
SERVES 4

400 ml / 15 fl oz sour cream
12 macaroons, crumbled
45 ml / 3 tbs sugar
1 medium-sized fresh pineapple,
peeled, cored and cut into chunks
2 oranges, peeled, pith removed and
sliced
225 g / 8 oz strawberries, washed,
hulled and halved
30 ml / 2 tbs brandy
30 ml / 2 tbs slivered almonds,
toasted

In a small mixing bowl, combine the sour cream, macaroons and sugar. Put the bowl in the refrigerator for 2 hours.

Layer the pineapple, oranges and strawberries with the sour cream mixture in a glass serving bowl. Sprinkle over the brandy and scatter the almonds over the top.

Serve immediately.

N.B. If strawberries are not available, grapes or raspberries may be used instead.

Lemon soufflé — cold
SERVES 6

5 egg yolks
125 g / 4 oz caster
sugar
Finely grated rind and juice of
3 lemons
15 g / ½ oz gelatin, dissolved in 60 ml
4 tbs hot water
300 ml / 10 fl oz double
cream
5 egg whites

In a medium-sized heatproof mixing bowl combine the egg yolks and sugar. Put the bowl over a saucepan half full of hot water. Place the pan over moderate heat and, using a wire whisk or rotary beater, beat the mixture for 15–20 minutes or until it is thick and pale.

Add the lemon rind and juice and continue beating until the mixture makes a ribbon trail on itself when the whisk is lifted.

Left: Pineapple filled with fresh fruit.

Alternatively beat the egg yolks, sugar and lemon rind for 5 minutes or until thick in an electric mixer. Add the lemon juice to the egg mixture and continue beating until the mixture makes a ribbon trail on itself when the beater is lifted.

Remove the bowl from the pan and set it in a large bowl or baking dish containing cold water. Continue whisking until the mixture and the bowl are quite cold.

Pour in the gelatin and stir well.

In a small mixing bowl, whip the cream with a wire whisk or rotary beater until it is thick but not stiff. Fold it into the egg and lemon mixture. Place the bowl in the refrigerator to chill for about 1 hour, or until the mixture is cold but not quite set.

Beat the egg whites with a wire whisk or rotary beater until they stand in stiff peaks and the bowl can be turned upside down without the egg whites falling out. Carefully fold the egg whites into the lemon mixture, then spoon into a decorative bowl or soufflé dish. Place in the refrigerator and chill for 4–5 hours, or until the soufflé is set.

Tropical fruit salad
SERVES 8

1 large pineapple
1 large orange, peeled, pith removed
and cut into segments
2 bananas, peeled and sliced
125 g / 4 oz black grapes, halved and
seeded
6 fresh passion fruit, tops removed
and the pulp squeezed out
1 ogen melon, peeled, seeded and
chopped
450 g / 16 oz canned pawpaws
450 g / 16 oz canned guavas
Juice of 1 orange
Juice of 1 lemon
125 ml / 4 fl oz orange-flavoured
liqueur

With a sharp knife, carefully cut off the top and a thin slice off the base of the pineapple. Discard the pineapple base but retain the top. Remove the flesh from the peel, leaving a 1.2 cm / ½ in thick shell. Set the pineapple shell aside.

Remove and discard the core from the pineapple flesh. Cut the flesh into small pieces and place them in a large mixing bowl. Add the orange, bananas, grapes, passion fruit, melon and pawpaw to the bowl. Strain the guavas through a wire strainer placed over a small mixing bowl and reserve the can juice. Add the guavas to the other fruits and set aside.

Add the orange and lemon juice and orange-flavoured liqueur to the can juice and stir well. Set aside.

Place the reserved pineapple shell, upright, in the centre of a large serving dish. Spoon two-thirds of the fruit mixture into the shell. Place the remaining fruit around the base of the pineapple. Pour the orange-flavoured liqueur mixture into the pineapple shell. Replace the reserved pineapple top and chill the dish in the refrigerator for 30 minutes or until required.

Remove the dish from the refrigerator and serve immediately, on its own or with fresh cream or ice cream.

Syllabub
SERVES 4–6
50 g / 2 oz sugar
Juice of 1 large lemon
Rind and juice of $\frac{1}{2}$ orange
90 ml / 6 tbs medium-dry sherry
30 ml / 2 tbs brandy
300 ml / 10 fl oz double cream, beaten until thick but not stiff

In a medium-sized mixing bowl, combine the sugar, lemon juice, orange rind and juice, sherry and brandy. Gradually pour the cream into the bowl, beating constantly until the ingredients are thoroughly combined.

Cover the bowl and chill it in the refrigerator for at least 30 minutes or until ready to serve.

Remove the bowl from the refrigerator and pour the syllabub into chilled individual serving dishes. Serve immediately.

N.B. A delightful dish that can be made in a moment, syllabub is a traditional English dessert. Serve either on its own in decorative glasses or with poached fruit or brandy snaps.

Sherbet
SERVES 4
225 g / 8 oz sugar
425 ml / 16 fl oz water
7.5 ml / 1$\frac{1}{2}$ tsp gelatin, dissolved in
30 ml / 2 tbs hot water
675 g / 1$\frac{1}{2}$ lb fresh raspberries, hulled
125 ml / 4 fl oz double cream
1 egg white, stiffly beaten

Set the thermostat of the refrigerator to its coldest setting.

In a medium-sized saucepan, dissolve

the sugar in the water over low heat, stirring constantly. Increase the heat to high and bring the syrup to the boil. Boil the syrup for 10–15 minutes or until the temperature reaches 104°C / 220°F on a sugar thermometer or a small amount dropped in cold water forms a short thread when pulled between thumb and index finger.

Remove the pan from the heat and set the syrup aside to cool for 5 minutes. Stir in the gelatin mixture.

Purée the raspberries in a blender and rub them through a strainer into a medium-sized mixing bowl. Alternatively, using the back of a wooden spoon, rub the raspberries through a strainer into a medium-sized mixing bowl. Stir in the syrup. Pour the mixture into a large mixing bowl. Cover the bowl and place it in the refrigerator to chill for 1 hour.

When the mixture is cold, spoon it into

Above: Sherbet is best made with fresh raspberries, but frozen ones also work.

a cold freezing-tray and put it into the freezer compartment of the refrigerator to freeze for 1 hour.

Meanwhile, in a small mixing bowl, using a wire whisk or rotary beater, beat the cream until it is thick but not stiff. Using a metal spoon, fold the beaten egg white into the cream.

Remove the tray from the refrigerator. Scrape the sherbet into a large mixing bowl. Using a wire whisk or rotary beater, beat the sherbet until it is smooth. Fold the cream mixture into the sherbet. Spoon the sherbet back into the tray and return the tray to the freezer compartment. Freeze for 6 hours or until the sherbet is firm to the touch.

Remove the sherbet from the freezer compartment. Spoon the sherbet into individual serving dishes and serve at once.

N.B. The puréed raspberries, fresh or frozen, should make about 600 ml / 1 pint in quantity; if they do not, make up the volume with water. Serve the sherbet either on its own or decorated with sugared fresh fruit.

Fruit ambrosia
SERVES 6
½ kg / 1 lb strawberries, washed and hulled
2 dessert apples, peeled, cored and coarsely chopped
Juice of 1 lemon
50 ml / 2 fl oz sweet white wine
225 g / 8 oz fresh apricots, peeled, stoned and coarsely chopped
45 ml / 3 tbs sugar
150 ml / 5 fl oz double cream, stiffly whipped

Put all the ingredients except the cream and six of the strawberries in a blender and blend, off and on, at high speed until the mixture is a smooth purée. Alternatively, the fruits may be puréed in a food mill. Taste and add more sugar, if desired.

Spoon the purée into six individual sundae glasses and place them in the refrigerator. Leave to chill for about 3 hours.

To serve, remove the sundae dishes from the refrigerator and decorate each serving with the whipped cream and reserved whole strawberries.

Syllabub trifle
SERVES 6–8
700 g / 1½ lb strawberries, washed, hulled and halved
3 ogen melons, flesh scooped out with a melon-baller (skins and seeds discarded)
275 g / 10 oz raspberries, hulled
275 g / 10 oz macaroons, crushed

225 g / 8 oz caster sugar
4 egg whites, stiffly beaten
400 ml / 15 fl oz double cream
300 ml / 10 fl oz dry white wine
Juice of ½ lemon
45 ml / 3 tbs brandy
12 whole strawberries, washed and hulled

In a large glass serving bowl, arrange a third of the strawberries. Cover the strawberries with a third of the melon balls and a third of the raspberries. Top with some of the crushed macaroons. Continue making layers in this way until all these ingredients are used up, ending with a layer of macaroons. Set aside.

Add a quarter of the sugar to the stiffly beaten egg whites and beat for 2 minutes. Using a metal spoon, carefully fold the remaining sugar into the egg white mixture. Set aside.

Pour the cream into a large mixing bowl and, using a wire whisk or rotary beater, beat the cream until it is thick but not stiff. Add the wine, lemon juice and brandy and beat just to mix well. Using a metal spoon, fold the egg white mixture into the cream. Spoon the cream mixture over the fruit mixture and place the bowl in the refrigerator to chill for at least 2 hours.

Remove the bowl from the refrigerator, arrange the whole strawberries on top and serve immediately.

INDEX

Barbecue party menus

For the children

California Cocktail
Mexican Stuffed Eggs
Hot Dog Kebabs
Corn-on-the-Cob in Foil
Coleslaw with Caraway
Pita
Strawberry Shortcake

An informal gathering

Sangria
Selection of Dips and Crudité
Spareribs with Sweet-and-Sour Sauce
Baked Potatoes in Foil
Spinach Salad
Garlic Bread
Kebabs with Fruit

Elegance in moonlight

Sparkling White Wine Cup
Cucumber and Mint Soup
Rotisseried Lamb with Coriander
and Garlic
Baked Potato in Foil
Foil-wrapped Courgettes
Mushroom and Mint Salad
Herb Bread Crisps
Syllabub

Pictures supplied by:
Bryce Atwell 1 and 20, 11, 14
Barry Bullough 17
Camera Press 21
Courtesy Le Creuset 6/7, 28/9
Alan Duns 18, 19, 22/3, 30, 56
Graeme Harris 9
Paul Kemp 19, 62
Don Last 4/5, 52
Key Nilson 49
PAF International/Delu 26, 39, 45, 48
Roger Phillips 15, 16, 24, 32/3, 34, 37, 38,
    41, 43, 47, 50, 53, 54, 57, 59, 60/1, 63
Spike Powell 27
Iain Reid 35
Kim Sayer 2
Malcolm Scoular 12
David Smith 40
Cover by Roger Phillips